The Cybersecurity Blueprint

Protecting Your Systems
Against Emerging Threats

THOMPSON CARTER

Table of Content

TABLE OF CONTENTS

INTRODUCTION

The Cybersecurity Blueprint

In an increasingly connected world, the digital frontier has expanded at an unprecedented rate. As our lives become more intertwined with technology, the very systems we rely on for communication, commerce, healthcare, and entertainment also face constant threats from malicious actors. Cybersecurity has never been more important. Today, it's not just a technical issue—it's a critical, universal concern that impacts individuals, businesses, governments, and societies alike. From **data breaches** to **ransomware attacks**, the growing complexity of cyber threats demands a proactive, comprehensive approach to defending our digital world.

In **The Cybersecurity Blueprint: Protecting Your Systems Against Emerging Threats**, we embark on an in-depth journey to understand the nature of modern cyber threats and how to build resilient, robust defenses against them. This book is designed for both **beginners** looking to enter the world of cybersecurity and **professionals** who want to sharpen their skills and stay ahead of evolving threats.

Throughout this book, you'll gain a thorough understanding of the many facets of cybersecurity, from its fundamental principles to the most advanced techniques for threat mitigation. Whether you're an individual looking to safeguard your personal data, a small business owner protecting valuable assets, or a professional tasked with securing enterprise networks, this guide will give you the tools and knowledge to defend against the ever-growing array of cyber risks.

23

Why Cybersecurity is Crucial Today

The digital landscape has grown more complex and interconnected, resulting in an expanding attack surface. Cybercriminals are no longer limited to traditional forms of hacking; they now have access to cutting-edge technologies like **AI**, **machine learning**, and **quantum computing** to carry out sophisticated attacks. These malicious actors have increasingly turned their attention to not just financial gain but also espionage, political agendas, and the disruption of critical infrastructures.

While the **Internet of Things (IoT)**, **cloud computing**, and **artificial intelligence** have revolutionized the way we live and work, they have also introduced new vulnerabilities. Data breaches, social engineering tactics, ransomware, and **Advanced Persistent Threats (APTs)** are now daily headlines. The security of personal data, private transactions, and national security is now directly tied to the integrity of the systems that support them.

As we navigate this evolving digital world, cybersecurity is no longer a one-time effort; it's an ongoing commitment to learning, adapting, and securing digital ecosystems in the face of ever-changing threats.

What This Book Will Cover

This book is structured to help you understand the principles, tools, and strategies needed to navigate the fast-paced and constantly evolving world of cybersecurity. Here's what you can expect:

1. **Foundational Concepts** – In the first section, we'll explore the fundamental principles of cybersecurity, such as **confidentiality, integrity**, and **availability (the CIA Triad)**. We'll discuss the role of encryption, firewalls, and the importance of having a layered defense strategy known as **Defense in Depth**.

2. **Emerging Threats and Attacks** – Cyber threats are growing in sophistication. We'll take a deep dive into **malware, ransomware, phishing**, and **Advanced Persistent Threats (APTs)**. We'll also look at new and emerging risks related to **cloud computing, IoT devices**, and **smart technology**.

3. **Cyber Defense Strategies** – Understanding how to protect yourself and your organization from these risks is key. This section will cover **network security, incident response**, and **disaster recovery**. We'll also dive into **real-time threat detection** and how **AI-driven security tools** can enhance your defenses.

4. **Hands-On Applications** – Throughout the book, we'll provide actionable insights and real-world examples that can be applied immediately. From setting up your **first firewall** to detecting **network intrusions** and writing **secure code**, we'll provide a practical roadmap to becoming a cybersecurity pro.

5. **Future Technologies in Cybersecurity** – Finally, we'll explore the future of cybersecurity. How will **AI, quantum computing**, and **blockchain** change the cybersecurity landscape? What will the next wave of threats look like, and how can we prepare for them?

Why This Book is Different

The landscape of cybersecurity is vast and complex, and it's easy to become overwhelmed by the amount of information available. **The Cybersecurity Blueprint** stands apart by offering a **clear, structured approach** to the subject. We go beyond theory and give you **real-world insights** and **practical applications** that can be implemented right away.

This book provides a **step-by-step framework** that helps you understand how each element of cybersecurity works, how to protect your systems, and how to recover if something goes wrong. With actionable tips, hands-on projects, and expert advice, you'll be equipped to tackle both current and future cybersecurity challenges.

Who This Book is For

This book is designed for **individuals** and **professionals** who want to learn how to protect their systems against the ever-growing range of cyber threats. Whether you're a **beginner** just starting out in cybersecurity or an experienced professional looking to deepen your knowledge, this book offers something for everyone.

- **Beginner-Level Readers** – If you're new to cybersecurity, you'll find foundational concepts that will help you build a solid understanding of the subject. Each chapter explains key concepts in simple, straightforward language.

- **Intermediate and Advanced Readers** – If you have experience in cybersecurity, you'll find **in-depth analyses** of advanced topics such as **AI-driven defense**, **network segmentation**, and **incident response strategies** that can help enhance your current skill set.
- **Business Owners and IT Professionals** – For those tasked with protecting a company's assets, this book provides guidance on **securing networks**, **protecting sensitive data**, and implementing an **enterprise-wide security strategy**.

Conclusion

As we move into the next decade, the threats we face in the digital world will continue to grow, but so too will our ability to defend against them. The tools, techniques, and strategies available to cybersecurity professionals are constantly evolving, and staying ahead of the curve is crucial.

In **The Cybersecurity Blueprint**, you'll gain the skills, knowledge, and confidence to **protect yourself** and **secure your systems** in an increasingly hostile digital environment. Whether you're protecting your personal data, securing a small business, or leading an enterprise security team, this book will provide you with the blueprint to build a **cybersecure future**.

The digital world is only becoming more interconnected—and with the right knowledge, you can ensure it remains safe, secure, and resilient against the threats of tomorrow.

CHAPTER 1

Introduction to Cybersecurity

Introduction

In an increasingly digital world, **cybersecurity** has become a crucial part of everyday life. From personal banking transactions to corporate data storage and national security, **protecting digital assets** is more important than ever.

But what exactly is cybersecurity? Why does it matter so much? And how do cyber threats evolve over time? In this chapter, we'll explore the foundations of cybersecurity, key attack surfaces, and real-world examples of **cyber breaches that changed industries**.

---

1. What is Cybersecurity and Why Does It Matter?

Defining Cybersecurity

At its core, **cybersecurity** is the practice of protecting systems, networks, and data from digital attacks, unauthorized access, and damage. It involves a combination of **technology, processes, and people** working together to safeguard information.

Cybersecurity encompasses:

- **Network Security** – Protecting networks from intrusions and malware.

- **Application Security** – Securing software and preventing vulnerabilities.
- **Data Security** – Encrypting and safeguarding sensitive data.
- **Operational Security** – Implementing best practices for handling digital assets.
- **Disaster Recovery & Business Continuity** – Ensuring recovery from cyber incidents.

Why Cybersecurity is Crucial

With the rapid expansion of digital technologies, cyber threats have grown exponentially. The risks of a **cyber attack** can be catastrophic, leading to:

1. **Financial Loss** – Cybercrimes cost companies billions of dollars annually.
2. **Reputation Damage** – A single breach can destroy consumer trust.
3. **Legal Consequences** – Companies may face lawsuits and regulatory fines.
4. **National Security Risks** – Government systems and critical infrastructure are frequent targets.

Real-World   Example:
In **2021, Colonial Pipeline**, the largest fuel pipeline in the U.S., suffered a **ransomware attack**, disrupting fuel supplies across the East Coast. The attackers demanded a ransom in Bitcoin, highlighting the economic and national security implications of cybersecurity failures.

---

2. The Rise of Cyber Threats in a Digital World

The Evolution of Cyber Attacks

Cyber threats have evolved significantly over the years. Early hacking efforts in the 1980s were mostly **harmless pranks**, but modern cyber attacks involve **sophisticated, state-sponsored campaigns** targeting businesses, governments, and individuals.

Decade	Cybersecurity Evolution
1980s-1990s	Early computer viruses and basic hacking attempts
2000s	Rise of phishing scams and large-scale data breaches
2010s	Nation-state cyber warfare, ransomware, and IoT attacks
2020s+	AI-powered attacks, cloud security threats, and advanced persistent threats (APTs)

Common Types of Cyber Threats

1. **Malware (Viruses, Worms, Trojans, Ransomware)** – Malicious software that can steal, encrypt, or destroy data.
2. **Phishing Attacks** – Fraudulent emails or messages designed to trick users into revealing sensitive information.
3. **Denial-of-Service (DoS) Attacks** – Overloading a system to make it inaccessible.
4. **Man-in-the-Middle (MitM) Attacks** – Intercepting and manipulating communication between two parties.
5. **Advanced Persistent Threats (APTs)** – Stealthy, prolonged cyberattacks by highly skilled attackers (often nation-states).

Who are the Attackers?

Cybercriminals come in various forms, each with different motivations:

- **Hacktivists** – Groups like Anonymous who hack for political or social reasons.
- **Cybercriminals** – Individuals or organizations seeking financial gain through cyber fraud.
- **Nation-State Hackers** – Government-backed hackers targeting foreign governments and corporations.
- **Insider Threats** – Employees or contractors who misuse their access to systems.

Real-World   Example:
The **2017 Equifax Data Breach** exposed personal data of **147 million people** due to an unpatched security vulnerability. Hackers exploited a known weakness, highlighting the risks of poor cybersecurity hygiene.

---

3. Understanding Attack Surfaces and Vulnerabilities

An **attack surface** refers to all the ways an attacker can exploit a system. The larger the attack surface, the **greater the risk of a cyber attack**.

Types of Attack Surfaces

1. **Digital Attack Surface** – Includes networks, applications, APIs, and databases.
2. **Physical Attack Surface** – Includes hardware devices, USB ports, and access control mechanisms.
3. **Human Attack Surface** – The risks associated with human error, weak passwords, and social engineering attacks.

Common Cybersecurity Vulnerabilities

- **Weak Passwords** – Many attacks succeed due to easily guessable or reused passwords.
- **Unpatched Software** – Failure to update software leaves systems exposed to known vulnerabilities.
- **Misconfigured Security Settings** – Improper configurations in firewalls, cloud environments, or databases can create security gaps.
- **Lack of Multi-Factor Authentication (MFA)** – Without MFA, a compromised password alone can allow unauthorized access.

Real-World   Example:
In **2019, Capital One** suffered a data breach affecting **100 million customers** due to a **misconfigured firewall** in their cloud infrastructure. A former employee exploited this weakness to steal sensitive data.

---

4. Real-World Cyber Breaches That Changed Industries

A. The Yahoo Data Breach (2013-2014)

- **What   Happened?**
  Over **3 billion user accounts** were compromised in one of the largest breaches in history.
- **How   Did   It   Happen?**
  Attackers gained access to weakly secured Yahoo systems using stolen credentials.
- **Impact:**
  Yahoo lost public trust, and the company's value significantly dropped during its acquisition by Verizon.

B. WannaCry Ransomware Attack (2017)

- **What   Happened?**
  The **WannaCry ransomware** attack infected **230,000**

computers worldwide, demanding ransom payments in Bitcoin.

- **How   Did   It   Happen?**
  Attackers exploited a known vulnerability in **Windows SMB protocol**.
- **Impact:**
  Hospitals, businesses, and governments worldwide suffered severe operational disruptions.

C. SolarWinds Cyber Espionage Attack (2020)

- **What   Happened?**
  A **nation-state cyber attack** compromised **SolarWinds**, affecting **U.S. government agencies and Fortune 500 companies**.
- **How   Did   It   Happen?**
  Attackers inserted a **backdoor** into a software update, allowing them to spy on organizations undetected.
- **Impact:**
  One of the most sophisticated cyber espionage campaigns in history, demonstrating the risks of **supply chain attacks**.

5. Key Takeaways

✔ **Cybersecurity is critical** in today's digital age, affecting everything from personal data to global security.
✔ **The cyber threat landscape is evolving**, with attackers using increasingly sophisticated tactics.
✔ **Understanding attack surfaces** helps organizations minimize risk and protect against cyber threats.
✔ **Real-world breaches** highlight the importance of cybersecurity best practices, from strong passwords to multi-factor authentication and regular software updates.

Next Chapter: The Cyber Threat Landscape

In **Chapter 2**, we'll dive deeper into the **cyber threat landscape**, exploring the different types of cyberattacks, who the attackers are, and how organizations can stay ahead of emerging threats.

Cybersecurity is a constantly evolving field—let's keep learning! 🚀

CHAPTER 2

Core Cybersecurity Principles

Introduction

Cybersecurity is more than just installing antivirus software or setting up firewalls—it's about adopting **foundational principles** that guide security policies, best practices, and decision-making. Every organization, from small businesses to large enterprises, needs to understand **core cybersecurity principles** to build a strong security posture.

In this chapter, we will explore:

- The **CIA Triad**: The three fundamental pillars of cybersecurity.
- **Defense in Depth**: A layered security strategy to mitigate threats.
- The **Zero Trust Model**: Why trust should never be assumed in cybersecurity.

By the end of this chapter, you'll have a deeper understanding of these principles and how they apply in real-world cybersecurity strategies.

---

1. The CIA Triad: The Three Pillars of Cybersecurity

The **CIA Triad** is a fundamental model in cybersecurity that consists of three principles:

Principle	Definition	Real-World Example
Confidentiality	Ensuring that information is accessible only to those who have authorized access.	Encrypted communication between a bank and its customers.
Integrity	Maintaining the accuracy and reliability of data.	Digital signatures prevent tampering in email communication.
Availability	Ensuring that systems and data are accessible when needed.	Cloud service providers ensuring uptime through redundancy.

A. Confidentiality: Protecting Sensitive Data

Confidentiality ensures that **only authorized users** can access sensitive data. Organizations implement confidentiality measures to prevent **unauthorized access, data breaches, and insider threats**.

How Confidentiality is Maintained:

- **Encryption**: Encrypting sensitive data ensures that even if it is intercepted, it remains unreadable. Example: **AES encryption for financial transactions**.
- **Access Control**: Restricting access based on user roles (Role-Based Access Control - RBAC). Example: Only HR employees can access payroll data.
- **Multi-Factor Authentication (MFA)**: Adds an extra layer of security beyond just a password. Example: Logging into an online bank account using both a password and a One-Time Passcode (OTP).

36

Real-World Example:

The **2019 Capital One Data Breach** exposed **100 million customer records** due to a **misconfigured firewall**. Attackers gained unauthorized access to **social security numbers, bank account details, and credit scores**. The breach highlights the need for **strict access control and encryption** to maintain confidentiality.

B. Integrity: Ensuring Accuracy and Trustworthiness of Data

Integrity means that **data should not be altered or tampered with**—whether in storage, in transit, or during processing. Cyber attackers often attempt to modify or delete critical data, which can have devastating effects.

How Integrity is Maintained:

- **Hashing Algorithms**: Hash functions like **SHA-256** generate unique fingerprints for data to verify its integrity. Example: Digital signatures for verifying document authenticity.
- **Checksums and Parity Bits**: Used in network transmissions to detect errors in data.
- **Audit Logs**: Track changes and unauthorized modifications.

Real-World Example:

In **2015, hackers targeted the Ukrainian power grid**, altering control settings and shutting down power stations. This attack compromised data integrity by modifying **control panel settings remotely**.

C. Availability: Ensuring Reliable Access to Information and Services

Availability ensures that **data and services are accessible whenever needed**, even during cyber attacks or system failures.

How Availability is Maintained:

- **Redundancy and Failover Systems**: Backup servers take over if primary systems fail.
- **Load Balancing**: Distributes traffic evenly across multiple servers to prevent overload.
- **DDoS Protection**: Firewalls and anti-DDoS services prevent attackers from overwhelming a website.

Real-World Example:

In **2021, Amazon Web Services (AWS) experienced an outage**, causing **major disruptions** for businesses using AWS for cloud computing. The incident highlighted the importance of **disaster recovery plans** and availability strategies.

2. Defense in Depth: Layered Security Strategies

Defense in Depth (DiD) is a cybersecurity approach that uses **multiple layers of security** to protect systems from attacks. Instead of relying on a single security measure, DiD ensures that **even if one layer fails, others remain active**.

A. The Multi-Layered Approach

Organizations implement multiple security layers, which can include:

Security Layer	Description
Physical Security	Secure access to data centers and restricted areas.
Network Security	Firewalls, VPNs, and intrusion detection systems (IDS).
Endpoint Security	Antivirus software, endpoint detection, and response (EDR).
Application Security	Secure coding practices, penetration testing.
Data Security	Encryption, backup solutions, and access controls.

B. Real-World Application of Defense in Depth

1. **Bank Security as an Analogy**: Imagine a bank protecting its money. It has **multiple layers of security**:
   o A **fence** around the bank (perimeter security).
   o **Locked doors and vaults** (physical security).
   o **CCTV cameras** (monitoring and detection).
   o **Security guards and authentication checks** (access control).
2. **Case Study: Target Data Breach (2013)**
   o Attackers **gained access through a third-party vendor**.
   o They installed **malware on the point-of-sale (POS) systems**.

o **Lack of layered security** allowed **40 million credit card records** to be stolen.

C. Best Practices for Implementing Defense in Depth

- **Use Firewalls and IDS**: Monitor incoming and outgoing traffic.
- **Apply Least Privilege Principle**: Give employees only the access they need.
- **Enforce Strong Authentication**: Require MFA for all critical systems.
- **Implement Security Awareness Training**: Train employees to recognize phishing attacks.

---

3. The Zero Trust Model: Never Trust, Always Verify

Traditional cybersecurity models assume that users **inside a network** are trustworthy. However, modern cyber threats **come from both external and internal sources**. The **Zero Trust Model** assumes that **no one should be trusted by default, regardless of whether they are inside or outside the network**.

A. Principles of Zero Trust

1. **Verify Explicitly** – Always authenticate users before granting access.
2. **Least Privilege Access** – Users should have **only the permissions they need**.
3. **Micro-Segmentation** – Divide networks into segments to limit movement.
4. **Continuous Monitoring** – Use AI and machine learning to detect anomalies.

B. Zero Trust in Action: Real-World Example

- In **2020, Twitter was hacked** by attackers who tricked employees into revealing their credentials.
- **Zero Trust could have prevented this** by enforcing multi-factor authentication (MFA) and requiring **additional verification** for high-privilege access.

C. Implementing Zero Trust

- **Adopt MFA**: Every access request should be verified using multiple factors.
- **Monitor Network Traffic**: Use **User and Entity Behavior Analytics (UEBA)** to detect anomalies.
- **Apply Strong Identity Management**: Use role-based access controls (RBAC) and secure credentials.

Key Takeaways

✔ **The CIA Triad (Confidentiality, Integrity, Availability)** is the foundation of cybersecurity.
✔ **Defense in Depth** provides multiple security layers to protect against cyber threats.
✔ **Zero Trust ensures that trust is never assumed—** access must be continuously verified.

By understanding and applying these cybersecurity principles, individuals and organizations can significantly reduce their risk of **data breaches, insider threats, and cyber attacks**.

Next Chapter: How Cyber Attacks Work - The Hacker's Playbook

In **Chapter 3**, we'll take a deep dive into **how hackers exploit vulnerabilities**, their **attack techniques**, and how cybersecurity professionals defend against them. Get ready to **think like a hacker to stop cyber threats!** 🚀

CHAPTER 3

How Cyber Attacks Work – The Hacker's Playbook

Introduction

Cyber attacks don't happen randomly. Hackers follow a structured **methodology** to infiltrate systems, exploit vulnerabilities, and achieve their goals—whether it's stealing data, disrupting services, or holding companies hostage with ransomware.

Understanding **how cyber attacks work** helps individuals and organizations defend against them. In this chapter, we'll explore:

- **Attack vectors** – The different ways hackers gain access to systems.
- **Exploiting vulnerabilities** – How attackers leverage weaknesses like social engineering and misconfigurations.
- **The Cyber Kill Chain** – A structured model that breaks down cyber attacks into predictable stages.
- **Real-world attack demonstrations** – Simulations that showcase how these attacks unfold.

By the end of this chapter, you'll have a **hacker's mindset**—not to attack, but to better defend.

1. Attack Vectors: How Hackers Gain Access to Systems

An **attack vector** is the method hackers use to exploit weaknesses in a system. The more attack vectors an organization has, the greater the security risk.

Common Attack Vectors

Attack Vector	Description	Example
Phishing	Deceptive emails trick users into revealing credentials.	Fake emails pretending to be from banks.
Malware	Malicious software that steals data or disrupts systems.	Ransomware encrypting corporate files.
Zero-Day Exploits	Attacks that exploit unknown vulnerabilities.	Unpatched security flaws in software.
Man-in-the-Middle (MitM) Attacks	Intercepting and altering communications.	Fake Wi-Fi networks used to steal login credentials.
Brute Force Attacks	Systematic guessing of passwords or encryption keys.	Automated bots trying thousands of password combinations.
SQL Injection	Injecting malicious SQL commands into a database.	A hacker retrieves sensitive customer data

Attack Vector	Description	Example
		from a vulnerable website.
Insider Threats	Malicious or negligent employees exposing systems.	Disgruntled employees selling company secrets.

Real-World Example: The Colonial Pipeline Ransomware Attack (2021)

In **May 2021**, attackers **exploited a single leaked password** to gain access to the Colonial Pipeline's network, launching a **ransomware attack** that shut down fuel supply across the U.S. East Coast. The company **paid $4.4 million** in ransom to restore operations.

☑ **Lesson:** Weak passwords and **lack of multi-factor authentication (MFA)** made the attack possible.

---

2. Exploiting Vulnerabilities: Social Engineering & Misconfigurations

Hackers don't always rely on **technical exploits**. Sometimes, the easiest way in is **manipulating people** (social engineering) or **taking advantage of poor system configurations**.

A. Social Engineering: Hacking the Human Mind

Social engineering attacks manipulate people into **revealing confidential information** or performing risky actions. These attacks **exploit human psychology** rather than technical flaws.

Common Social Engineering Attacks

1. **Phishing** – Fraudulent emails tricking users into clicking malicious links or downloading malware.
2. **Vishing (Voice Phishing)** – Attackers posing as tech support, banks, or executives to extract information.
3. **Pretexting** – A fabricated scenario used to trick someone into giving up information.
4. **Baiting** – Leaving infected USB drives in public places, hoping someone plugs them into their computer.

Example:
In 2016, a **Google Docs phishing attack** tricked thousands of users into **granting hackers access to their Gmail accounts**. The attack was **so realistic** that even tech-savvy users fell for it.

☑ **Defense:** Train employees to **spot phishing** and never open suspicious links or attachments.

B. Misconfigurations: Leaving the Door Open

A **misconfiguration** occurs when a system, server, or application is improperly set up, exposing it to cyber threats.

Examples of Misconfigurations:

1. **Publicly Exposed Cloud Storage** – Databases stored in AWS S3 buckets without authentication.

2. **Weak Passwords & Default Credentials** – Many users never change default passwords, making them easy to exploit.
3. **Open Ports & Unpatched Systems** – Attackers scan the internet for **unprotected systems** running outdated software.

Real-World Example: Facebook Data Leak (2021)
In **April 2021**, a **misconfigured database** exposed **533 million Facebook users' data**—including phone numbers and email addresses. No hacking was required; the data was simply left unprotected.

☑ **Defense:** Implement **security hardening practices** and ensure **regular security audits**.

---

3. The Cyber Kill Chain: Stages of a Cyber Attack

The **Cyber Kill Chain**, developed by Lockheed Martin, breaks cyber attacks into **predictable stages**, helping security teams detect and stop attacks.

Stages of a Cyber Attack

Stage	Description	Real-World Example
1. Reconnaissance	Hackers research targets, looking for vulnerabilities.	Attackers scan company websites for exposed data.

Stage	Description	Real-World Example
2. Weaponization	Malware or exploits are created for the target.	A phishing email is crafted with malicious attachments.
3. Delivery	The attack is delivered to the victim (e.g., email, drive-by download).	A user receives a fake invoice email containing malware.
4. Exploitation	The hacker gains access by exploiting vulnerabilities.	A user unknowingly executes a malicious file.
5. Installation	A backdoor or persistent malware is installed.	A trojan is installed, allowing remote access.
6. Command & Control (C2)	The attacker controls the compromised system remotely.	The hacker exfiltrates sensitive files from a corporate network.
7. Actions on Objectives	The final goal: data theft, ransomware deployment, etc.	Ransomware encrypts company files, demanding payment.

Real-World Example: WannaCry Ransomware (2017)

- **Reconnaissance:** Hackers scanned the internet for unpatched Windows computers.

- **Weaponization:** A self-replicating worm (WannaCry) was developed.
- **Delivery:** The malware was spread via email and infected networks.
- **Exploitation & Installation:** WannaCry **exploited an unpatched vulnerability (EternalBlue).**
- **Command & Control:** The ransomware spread across organizations.
- **Actions on Objectives: 300,000 computers** were encrypted, and ransom was demanded.

✅ **Defense:** Keep **systems patched**, enforce **network segmentation**, and **use endpoint protection**.

---

4. Real-World Attack Demonstrations (Safe Simulations)

Understanding cyber attacks **through real-world simulations** helps us learn **how hackers operate**. Below are **two safe simulations** that demonstrate common attacks.

A. Phishing Attack Simulation

◆ **Objective:** Understand how phishing attacks work.
◆ **Simulation Steps:**

1. Go to https://gophish.com/ (a phishing training tool).
2. Set up a **fake phishing email campaign** to see how many users fall for it.
3. Analyze the results to **train employees** on detecting phishing.

B. Password Cracking Demonstration

◆ **Objective:** Show how weak passwords are cracked.
◆ **Simulation Steps:**

1. Download **Hashcat** (a legal password-cracking tool).
2. Create a **hashed password** and attempt to crack it using **common wordlists**.
3. Learn why **strong passwords and multi-factor authentication (MFA)** are crucial.

Key Takeaways

✔ **Hackers use multiple attack vectors**, including **phishing, malware, and brute-force attacks**.
✔ **Social engineering** and **misconfigurations** are major security   risks.
✔ The **Cyber Kill Chain** helps security teams detect and stop   attacks   before   they   escalate.
✔ **Real-world attack demonstrations** highlight why strong cybersecurity practices are essential.

Next Chapter: Cyber Hygiene – Everyday Security Practices

In **Chapter 4**, we'll explore **practical security habits** that individuals and organizations can implement to protect against cyber attacks.

Want to stay one step ahead of hackers? Mastering cyber hygiene is the first step. Let's dive in!

CHAPTER 4

The Cyber Threat Landscape – Understanding Your Enemies

Introduction

The cyber threat landscape is constantly evolving, with **attackers developing new techniques** to exploit individuals, businesses, and even governments. Cyber threats range from **malware and phishing attacks** to **ransomware campaigns and state-sponsored cyber warfare**.

In this chapter, we will explore:

- **Types of cyber threats** – How malware, phishing, ransomware, and Advanced Persistent Threats (APTs) work.
- **Who are the attackers?** – Understanding the motives and tactics of cybercriminals, nation-state actors, and insider threats.
- **Real-world cyber attacks** – Case studies that reveal **how attackers operate** and what lessons we can learn.

By the end of this chapter, you will have a deeper understanding of the cyber threat landscape and the **key risks organizations and individuals face today**.

1. Types of Cyber Threats

Cyber threats come in various forms, each with different methods and impacts. The most common threats include **malware, phishing, ransomware, and APTs**.

A. Malware: The Digital Parasite

Malware (malicious software) is a broad term covering software designed to infiltrate, damage, or steal information from systems.

Common Types of Malware:

Type	Description	Example
Viruses	Self-replicating programs that attach to files and spread.	ILOVEYOU virus (2000)
Worms	Spread automatically through networks without human interaction.	WannaCry (2017)
Trojans	Disguised as legitimate software but secretly execute harmful actions.	Zeus banking trojan
Spyware	Secretly monitors user activity and steals sensitive information.	Pegasus spyware
Keyloggers	Record keystrokes to steal passwords and other sensitive data.	Used in cyber espionage
Rootkits	Hide deep within the OS to give attackers persistent access.	Stuxnet (2010)

Real-World Example: WannaCry Ransomware Attack (2017)

- **Attack Method:** WannaCry spread using a Windows SMB vulnerability called **EternalBlue**.
- **Impact:** Infected **300,000 computers** in **150 countries**, shutting down hospitals and businesses.
- **Lesson:** Regular **patching and updates** could have prevented this attack.

B. Phishing: The Human Exploit

Phishing is a form of **social engineering** where attackers trick users into revealing sensitive information, such as login credentials or financial data.

Types of Phishing Attacks:

1. **Email Phishing** – Fake emails disguised as legitimate messages (e.g., from banks or tech support).
2. **Spear Phishing** – Targeted attacks aimed at specific individuals (e.g., CEOs, employees).
3. **Whaling** – High-level phishing targeting executives and government officials.
4. **Vishing (Voice Phishing)** – Fraudulent phone calls impersonating companies.
5. **Smishing (SMS Phishing)** – Fake text messages containing malicious links.

Real-World Example: Google & Facebook Phishing Attack (2013-2015)

- **Attack Method:** A hacker impersonated a vendor and sent fraudulent invoices to Google and Facebook.
- **Impact:** The scam resulted in **$100 million in stolen funds** before being detected.

- **Lesson:** Organizations need **strict financial verification processes** to prevent payment fraud.

C. Ransomware: Holding Data Hostage

Ransomware is malware that **encrypts a victim's files** and demands a ransom payment to restore access.

How Ransomware Works:

1. The attacker delivers ransomware through **phishing emails** or **exploited vulnerabilities**.
2. The malware **encrypts files** and locks access to systems.
3. The victim is presented with a **ransom demand**, often in **Bitcoin or Monero**.
4. If the ransom is paid, the attacker **may (or may not)** provide the decryption key.

Notorious Ransomware Attacks:

Attack Name	Year	Impact
WannaCry	2017	Affected 300,000+ computers worldwide.
NotPetya	2017	Caused $10 billion in damages.
Colonial Pipeline	2021	Shut down U.S. fuel supply for days.

Real-World Example: Colonial Pipeline Ransomware Attack (2021)

- **Attack Method:** Attackers exploited a **leaked VPN password** to gain network access.

- **Impact:** The attack **shut down fuel supply** across the U.S. East Coast for days.
- **Lesson: Multi-Factor Authentication (MFA)** could have prevented unauthorized access.

D. Advanced Persistent Threats (APTs): Cyber Espionage and Nation-State Attacks

An **Advanced Persistent Threat (APT)** is a long-term cyber attack by **highly skilled threat actors** (often nation-states) who aim to **steal data, disrupt operations, or conduct espionage**.

Characteristics of APTs:

- **Highly Sophisticated** – Attackers use custom malware and advanced hacking techniques.
- **Long-Term Intrusions** – APTs can remain undetected for **months or years**.
- **Targeted Attacks** – Focus on governments, corporations, and critical infrastructure.

Real-World Example: SolarWinds Cyber Espionage Attack (2020)

- **Attack Method:** Hackers inserted a **backdoor into a software update** for SolarWinds.
- **Impact:** The attack **compromised U.S. government agencies** and **Fortune 500 companies**.
- **Lesson: Supply chain security** is critical—third-party vendors must be rigorously vetted.

2. Who Are the Attackers? Understanding Cybercriminals

Cyber attackers come in different forms, with different **motivations and targets**.

Type of Attacker	Motivation	Example
Cybercriminals	Financial gain	Ransomware gangs demanding Bitcoin.
Hacktivists	Political or social activism	Anonymous launching DDoS attacks.
Insider Threats	Employees misusing access	A rogue employee selling customer data.
Nation-State Actors	Cyber warfare & espionage	China, Russia, North Korea engaging in APTs.

A. Cybercriminals: Hacking for Profit

Cybercriminals operate like **businesses**, using hacking as a means to generate income. Their primary methods include:

- **Ransomware-as-a-Service (RaaS)** – Selling ransomware kits to other criminals.
- **Dark Web Marketplaces** – Selling stolen credit cards, personal data, and hacking tools.
- **Bank Fraud & Identity Theft** – Stealing financial information and selling it online.

B. Hacktivists: Cyber Attacks for Political or Social Causes

Hacktivists use cyber attacks to **make political statements**. Their activities often include:

- **DDoS Attacks** – Overloading websites to shut them down.
- **Data Leaks** – Exposing confidential government or corporate documents.

Example:
The **Anonymous collective** has targeted governments and corporations in retaliation for perceived injustices.

C. Insider Threats: The Enemy Within

An **insider threat** is a person **within an organization** who **abuses their access** to steal data or sabotage systems.

Types of Insider Threats:

- **Malicious Insiders** – Employees intentionally harming their organization.
- **Negligent Insiders** – Employees who unintentionally expose sensitive information.

Example:
In 2018, an **Apple employee was caught stealing trade secrets** related to self-driving car technology.

---

3. Real-World Cyber Attacks and What We Learned

Attack	Year	Lesson Learned
Equifax Data Breach	2017	Keeping software updated is critical.

Attack	Year	Lesson Learned
Marriott Hotel Hack	2018	Weak third-party security can lead to major breaches.
Twitter Hack	2020	Social engineering attacks can bypass technical defenses.

Each of these cyber attacks demonstrates **the importance of strong security measures, employee training, and proactive threat management**.

Key Takeaways

✔ **Cyber threats come in many forms**, including malware, phishing, ransomware, and APTs.
✔ **Hackers have different motivations**, from financial gain to political activism.
✔ **Real-world cyber attacks highlight the importance of cybersecurity best practices** like MFA, software updates, and network segmentation.

Next Chapter: Cyber Hygiene — Everyday Security Practices

In **Chapter 5**, we'll focus on **practical steps** to protect yourself and your organization from cyber threats. **Being aware of threats is not enough—security requires action!** Let's dive into cybersecurity best practices next. 🚀

CHAPTER 5

Cyber Hygiene – Everyday Security Practices

Introduction

Good **cyber hygiene** is the first line of defense against cyber threats. Just like **personal hygiene** helps prevent illness, cyber hygiene protects digital assets from attacks. Many high-profile cyber breaches result from **poor security habits**, making it essential for individuals and businesses to follow cybersecurity best practices.

In this chapter, we'll cover:

- **The basics of cyber hygiene** – Password security, multi-factor authentication (MFA), and software updates.
- **Securing personal devices** – Protecting phones, laptops, and Internet of Things (IoT) devices.
- **Real-world example** – How a weak password led to a **multi-million-dollar breach**.

By the end of this chapter, you'll understand how small security habits can **prevent major cyber incidents**.

---

1. The Basics of Cyber Hygiene

A **strong cybersecurity foundation** starts with everyday security habits. The **most common cyber threats**, such as **phishing, malware, and data breaches**, often succeed due to **simple mistakes** like weak passwords or failing to install updates.

A. Password Security: The First Line of Defense

Passwords are **one of the weakest links** in cybersecurity. Many people **reuse passwords** across multiple accounts, making them an easy target for hackers.

Why Weak Passwords Are Dangerous

- **Most users use simple passwords** – "123456", "password", and "qwerty" are still among the most commonly used passwords.
- **Credential stuffing attacks** – Hackers use stolen usernames and passwords from one breach to break into other accounts.
- **Brute-force attacks** – Attackers use automated tools to guess passwords.

Best Practices for Password Security

✅ **Use Strong, Unique Passwords** – Each account should have a unique password with **at least 12–16 characters**, mixing uppercase, lowercase, numbers, and symbols.

✅ **Enable Password Managers** – Tools like **Bitwarden, 1Password, and LastPass** generate and store strong passwords securely.

✅ **Avoid Personal Information** – Don't use birthdays, pet names, or favorite sports teams in passwords.

✅ **Regularly Change Important Passwords** – Update passwords for financial accounts, email, and admin access **at least once a year**.

60

B. Multi-Factor Authentication (MFA): An Extra Layer of Protection

Even strong passwords can be stolen through **phishing or data breaches**. **Multi-Factor Authentication (MFA)** adds a **second layer of security**, making it **much harder** for hackers to gain access.

Types of MFA:

1. **SMS-Based Authentication** – A one-time code is sent via text message.
2. **Authenticator Apps (Best Option!)** – Apps like **Google Authenticator or Authy** generate time-based one-time passcodes (TOTP).
3. **Biometric Authentication** – Uses **fingerprints or facial recognition** (e.g., Apple Face ID, Windows Hello).
4. **Hardware Security Keys** – Physical devices like **YubiKey** provide the most secure MFA option.

☑ **Always enable MFA on:**

- Banking and financial accounts.
- Work and email accounts.
- Social media accounts.

📌 **Real-World Example: The Twitter Hack (2020)** Hackers **compromised high-profile Twitter accounts**, including **Elon Musk, Bill Gates, and Apple**, by using **social engineering** to trick employees into resetting passwords.
Lesson: MFA would have prevented unauthorized access!

C. Software & System Updates: Patching Security Holes

Many cyber attacks exploit **outdated software** that contains **known vulnerabilities**. If software isn't updated regularly, hackers can **easily exploit** security gaps.

Why Updates Matter:

- **Patching Vulnerabilities** – Updates fix known security flaws before hackers can exploit them.
- **Improved Security Features** – New versions of software often include better encryption and protection.
- **Automatic Updates Reduce Human Error** – Many cyber breaches occur because users delay or ignore updates.

✅ **Best Practices for Updates:**

- **Enable Automatic Updates** for your OS, browsers, and apps.
- **Update IoT devices** (smart TVs, routers, cameras) regularly.
- **Use Supported Software** – Don't use outdated software that no longer receives security updates.

📌 **Real-World Example: The Equifax Data Breach (2017)**
A **failure to install a security update** led to a **massive data breach** at **Equifax**, exposing **147 million customers' personal data**. The vulnerability had been **publicly disclosed two months before the breach**, but the company failed to update its systems.
Lesson: Delaying updates can cost millions in damages.

2. Securing Personal Devices: Phones, Laptops, and IoT

Cyber hygiene isn't just about **online security**—your **devices themselves** can be compromised if not properly secured.

A. Securing Smartphones

Smartphones contain **banking details, personal messages, and login credentials**, making them a prime target for cybercriminals.

✅ Tips to Protect Your Smartphone:

- **Use Strong Screen Locks** – PIN codes, biometrics, or complex passcodes.
- **Enable Remote Wipe** – Features like **Find My iPhone (Apple)** or **Find My Device (Android)** allow remote wiping if lost or stolen.
- **Install Apps from Trusted Sources** – Only download from **Google Play Store or Apple App Store**.
- **Avoid Public Wi-Fi for Sensitive Transactions** – Use **VPNs** to encrypt data when browsing on public networks.

📌 **Real-World Example: Pegasus Spyware (2019-Present)**
Pegasus spyware was used to **hack journalists, activists, and politicians** through **zero-click exploits** in iPhones and Android devices. Victims didn't even need to **click a link** to be infected.
Lesson: Keep devices updated and avoid clicking unknown links.

B. Laptop & Desktop Security

Laptops and desktops are commonly targeted by **malware, ransomware, and phishing attacks**.

✅ Best Practices:

- **Enable Full-Disk Encryption** – Protects data if a device is stolen.
- **Use a Secure Web Browser** – Chrome and Firefox offer **security features** like **anti-tracking and HTTPS enforcement**.
- **Run Security Software** – Antivirus and anti-malware tools like **Windows Defender, Malwarebytes, or Bitdefender**.

C. Protecting Internet of Things (IoT) Devices

IoT devices (smart TVs, home assistants, cameras, and routers) **often lack security measures**, making them an easy target.

Common IoT Security Risks:

- **Weak or Default Passwords** – Many IoT devices ship with **default passwords** that are easy to guess.
- **No Software Updates** – Some IoT devices rarely receive security patches.
- **Unsecured Network Access** – IoT devices may connect to the internet **without proper authentication**.

✅ Best Practices for IoT Security:

- **Change Default Passwords** on all devices.
- **Disable Unnecessary Features** like remote access if not needed.

- **Segment IoT Devices** on a separate network (e.g., use a **guest Wi-Fi** for IoT devices).

📌 **Real-World Example: Mirai Botnet (2016)** Hackers **infected thousands of IoT devices** (like security cameras and routers) with malware, creating the **Mirai botnet**, which launched one of the **largest DDoS attacks** in history.
Lesson: Unsecured IoT devices can be used in massive cyber attacks.

3. Real-World Example: How a Weak Password Led to a Multi-Million Dollar Breach

◆ **Case Study: The Colonial Pipeline Attack (2021)**

- Attackers gained access to the **Colonial Pipeline network** using a **single compromised VPN password**.
- The attack **shut down fuel distribution** on the U.S. East Coast for **several days**.
- The company **paid a $4.4 million ransom** to regain access.

◆ **What Went Wrong?**
✗ **No Multi-Factor Authentication (MFA)** on the VPN account.
✗ **Password reuse** – The password had been leaked in **a previous data breach.**

◆ **Lessons Learned:**
✅ **Always enable MFA** on critical accounts.
✅ **Use unique passwords** for each account.

65

☑ **Monitor for leaked credentials** using tools like **Have I Been Pwned**.

Key Takeaways

✔ **Cyber hygiene is essential** for preventing cyber attacks.

✔ **Strong passwords and multi-factor authentication (MFA)** protect accounts from hacking.

✔ **Regular software updates prevent attackers from exploiting known vulnerabilities.**

✔ **Personal devices and IoT security** are crucial for maintaining digital safety.

Next Chapter: Network Security — Keeping Attackers Out

In **Chapter 6**, we'll explore **network security best practices**, including **firewalls, VPNs, intrusion detection systems (IDS), and secure Wi-Fi configurations**.

🔒 **A secure network is a hacker's worst nightmare— let's build one!** 🚀

CHAPTER 6

Network Security – Keeping Attackers Out

Introduction

A secure network is the **foundation of cybersecurity**. Hackers often target **poorly secured networks** to infiltrate systems, steal data, or launch attacks. Many high-profile cyber breaches occur because **organizations fail to secure their networks properly**.

In this chapter, we'll explore:

- **Firewalls, VPNs, and IDS/IPS** – Key tools that help protect networks from unauthorized access.
- **Securing Wi-Fi networks** – Best practices to prevent hackers from exploiting weak wireless security.
- **Real-world case study** – How a **major corporation's weak network security** led to a cyber disaster.

By the end of this chapter, you'll understand **how to fortify your network against cyber threats**.

---

1. Firewalls, VPNs, and IDS/IPS Explained

A. Firewalls: The First Line of Defense

A **firewall** is a **security barrier** that **monitors and filters incoming and outgoing network traffic** based on security rules. It acts as a **gatekeeper**, allowing only legitimate traffic while blocking unauthorized connections.

Types of Firewalls:

Type	Description	Example Use Case
Packet-Filtering Firewall	Examines data packets and blocks suspicious ones based on rules.	Small businesses filtering traffic on routers.
Stateful Inspection Firewall	Tracks active connections and filters traffic based on session data.	Protecting corporate networks from unauthorized access.
Proxy Firewall	Acts as an intermediary between users and the internet.	Hides internal systems from the public internet.
Next-Gen Firewall (NGFW)	Includes deep packet inspection, intrusion detection, and malware filtering.	Enterprises securing cloud and on-premise environments.

✅ **Best Practices for Firewalls:**

- **Enable firewalls on all devices** (routers, servers, endpoints).
- **Regularly update firewall rules** to block new threats.
- **Use application-layer filtering** to detect malicious web traffic.

📌 **Real-World Example:** In **2019, a misconfigured firewall** allowed hackers to breach **Capital One**, exposing **100 million customer**

records.
Lesson: Firewalls must be properly configured and regularly tested.

B. Virtual Private Networks (VPNs): Secure Remote Access

A **VPN (Virtual Private Network)** encrypts internet connections, making it difficult for hackers or governments to intercept sensitive data.

Why Use a VPN?

- **Encrypts Internet Traffic** – Prevents hackers from spying on your online activities.
- **Protects Data on Public Wi-Fi** – Shields information from cybercriminals on untrusted networks.
- **Bypasses Geolocation Restrictions** – Enables access to region-restricted websites securely.

Corporate vs. Consumer VPNs

VPN Type	Purpose	Example
Corporate VPN	Secures remote work connections to company networks.	Employees accessing internal systems from home.
Consumer VPN	Protects individual privacy online.	NordVPN, ExpressVPN, ProtonVPN.

✅ **Best Practices for VPN Use:**

69

- **Use only trusted, no-log VPNs** to ensure privacy.
- **Avoid free VPNs**, as they may log and sell user data.
- **Require VPN access for remote employees** to protect company data.

📌 **Real-World Example:** In **2021, the Colonial Pipeline attack** occurred because a hacker **stole a VPN password** that had **no multi-factor authentication (MFA)** enabled. The result? A **shutdown of fuel distribution across the U.S. East Coast. Lesson: VPNs must be secured with strong authentication.**

C. Intrusion Detection & Prevention Systems (IDS/IPS)

Firewalls alone **can't detect all cyber threats**. This is where **Intrusion Detection Systems (IDS) and Intrusion Prevention Systems (IPS)** come into play.

IDS vs. IPS: What's the Difference?

System	Function	Example
IDS (Intrusion Detection System)	Monitors network traffic and alerts security teams of suspicious activity.	A system logging unauthorized login attempts.
IPS (Intrusion Prevention System)	Automatically blocks malicious traffic before it reaches the network.	Preventing DDoS attacks in real-time.

☑ **Best Practices for IDS/IPS:**

- **Use IDS to monitor traffic logs** and detect anomalies.
- **Deploy IPS to automatically block known threats**.
- **Regularly update threat intelligence databases** to detect new attack patterns.

📌 **Real-World Example:** A **financial institution used an IDS** to detect unauthorized access attempts. However, **without an IPS**, they failed to block an attack in time, resulting in **millions of stolen customer records**.
Lesson: A proactive IPS is better than relying on detection alone.

---

2. Securing Wi-Fi Networks and Preventing Unauthorized Access

Wireless networks are **high-risk attack surfaces** because they can be accessed remotely by hackers if not properly secured.

A. Wi-Fi Security Risks

- **Weak Passwords** – Many people use default or simple passwords like "123456" or "admin."
- **WPA2 Vulnerabilities** – Older encryption protocols (WEP, WPA) are **easily hackable**.
- **Rogue Access Points** – Hackers set up fake Wi-Fi networks to steal user data.

B. Best Practices for Wi-Fi Security

✅ **Use Strong WPA3 Encryption** – WPA3 is the latest, most secure encryption protocol.
✅ **Change Default Router Credentials** – Admin

71

usernames and passwords must be updated.
☑ **Disable WPS (Wi-Fi Protected Setup)** – WPS is vulnerable to brute-force attacks.
☑ **Use a Separate Guest Network** – Keep visitors isolated from company or personal devices.
☑ **Hide SSID (Optional)** – Prevents the Wi-Fi network from being publicly visible.

📌 **Real-World Example:** In **2018, a major U.K. airline** suffered a **customer data breach** because hackers **intercepted transactions via unsecured Wi-Fi connections**.
Lesson: Sensitive transactions should never be conducted over public Wi-Fi.

---

3. Case Study: A Major Corporation's Failure to Secure Its Network

Target Data Breach (2013)

One of the most infamous cybersecurity failures was the **Target breach**, where hackers stole **40 million credit card records**.

How Did It Happen?

1. **Network Segmentation Failure** – Hackers infiltrated the **HVAC system** used by a third-party vendor.
2. **Lateral Movement** – Attackers moved from the vendor system into Target's **payment processing network**.
3. **Data Exfiltration** – Payment card data was extracted **without triggering an alarm**.

Key Lessons from the Target Hack

✗ **No network segmentation** – The HVAC vendor should not have had access to payment systems.

✗ **Failure to monitor security alerts** – FireEye detected the intrusion **weeks before the attack**, but no action was taken.

☑ **Implement network segmentation** – Sensitive data should always be **isolated from third-party systems**.

☑ **Act on security alerts immediately** – **Ignoring red flags can lead to massive breaches.**

Key Takeaways

✔ **Firewalls, VPNs, and IDS/IPS are essential tools** for securing networks.

✔ **Wi-Fi security is often overlooked** but is a major attack surface for hackers.

✔ **A failure to secure networks properly** can lead to catastrophic breaches, as seen in the **Target data breach and Colonial Pipeline attack**.

Next Chapter: Endpoint Security – Protecting Devices from Attacks

In **Chapter 7**, we'll dive into **how to secure endpoints (laptops, desktops, and mobile devices)**, covering **antivirus software, EDR solutions, and access controls**.

🔒 A secure network is only as strong as its weakest device. Let's lock them down! 🚀

CHAPTER 7

Endpoint Security – Protecting Devices from Attacks

Introduction

Every day, organizations and individuals rely on **endpoints**—laptops, desktops, smartphones, and tablets—to access corporate networks, communicate, and store sensitive data. However, **endpoints are prime targets** for cybercriminals because they often lack proper security controls.

Hackers exploit **unprotected endpoints** to launch attacks, steal data, and deploy malware. A single **compromised employee laptop** can lead to a **massive data breach** or **ransomware infection**.

In this chapter, we'll cover:

- **Anti-malware & EDR solutions** – How modern security tools detect and block threats.
- **Controlling user privileges & application security** – Why **least privilege access** is critical.
- **Real-world attack scenario** – How a **compromised laptop** led to a **major cyber incident**.

By the end of this chapter, you'll understand **how to protect endpoints** against **malware, ransomware, phishing, and unauthorized access**.

1. Anti-Malware & EDR Solutions

A. Traditional Antivirus vs. Modern Endpoint Security

For years, **antivirus software** was the primary defense against malware. However, today's threats **evolve too quickly** for traditional antivirus to keep up. **Modern endpoint security solutions use AI-driven threat detection and behavioral analysis** to catch attacks in real time.

Security Solution	How It Works	Effectiveness
Antivirus (AV)	Uses a **signature-based** approach to detect known malware.	Good for **basic protection,** but ineffective against new threats.
Anti-Malware	Detects and removes **a wider range of threats,** including spyware and adware.	More advanced than antivirus but still **limited against sophisticated attacks**.
Endpoint Detection & Response (EDR)	Uses **AI, behavioral analysis, and threat intelligence** to detect and respond to **advanced cyber threats**.	Highly effective for **real-time attack detection and response**.

B. How EDR Improves Endpoint Security

EDR is **the modern approach to endpoint security**. Unlike traditional antivirus, **EDR continuously monitors, detects, and responds to security threats in real time**.

Key Features of EDR:

- **Real-Time Threat Monitoring** – Identifies suspicious activity on endpoints.
- **Automated Response** – Blocks threats before they cause damage.
- **Forensic Analysis** – Helps security teams investigate attacks.

✅ Top EDR Solutions:

- **Microsoft Defender for Endpoint**
- **CrowdStrike Falcon**
- **SentinelOne**
- **Carbon Black**

📌 **Real-World Example:** In 2021, **a major financial institution** detected **unusual activity on an employee's laptop**. Their **EDR system flagged a suspicious process**, revealing that **an attacker was attempting to install a keylogger**. The **attack was stopped before any data was stolen**. **Lesson: EDR solutions help detect threats that traditional antivirus would miss.**

---

2. Controlling User Privileges & Application Security

Many cyber attacks succeed because **users have excessive privileges**, allowing malware to spread quickly. A **least privilege access model** significantly reduces the risk.

A. The Principle of Least Privilege (PoLP)

The **Principle of Least Privilege (PoLP)** states that **users should have only the minimum permissions required to perform their tasks**.

Why PoLP is Critical:

- **Reduces Attack Surface** – If a hacker compromises a user's account, they **cannot access critical systems**.
- **Prevents Insider Threats** – Limits damage that a malicious or negligent employee can cause.
- **Stops Malware from Spreading** – Ransomware needs admin privileges to encrypt files.

✅ Best Practices for Least Privilege Access:

- **Limit Administrator Accounts** – Only **IT teams** should have admin rights.
- **Use Role-Based Access Control (RBAC)** – Employees only get access to **the tools they need**.
- **Monitor Privileged Accounts** – Log all admin activities to detect **suspicious behavior**.

📌 **Real-World Example:** In 2020, an **insider at Tesla** attempted to **deploy malware** into the company's network. However, Tesla's **strict access controls prevented the attacker from escalating privileges**, and the attack was **stopped before it could cause harm**.
Lesson: Strict privilege management prevents both insider and external attacks.

B. Application Security: Preventing Unsafe Software

Attackers often exploit **insecure applications** to gain access to systems. Weak applications provide **attack vectors** for malware, keyloggers, and ransomware.

Best Practices for Application Security:

✅ **Use Application Whitelisting** – Allow only **approved software** to run.
✅ **Keep Software Updated** – Unpatched applications are a major security risk.
✅ **Scan for Vulnerabilities** – Use tools like **Nessus** to detect weaknesses.

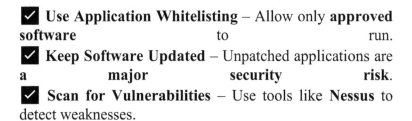 **Real-World Example:** In **2017, the NotPetya ransomware attack** spread through **unpatched Microsoft software**, crippling **global shipping and logistics companies**. **Lesson: Regular software updates prevent attackers from exploiting known vulnerabilities.**

3. Real-World Attack Scenario: A Compromised Employee Laptop

Case Study: How One Laptop Led to a Major Breach

The Attack:

A **marketing employee** at a **Fortune 500 company** was working remotely. They:

1. **Used a weak password** that had been leaked in a previous data breach.
2. **Did not have MFA enabled** on their corporate email account.
3. **Clicked on a phishing email** disguised as a Zoom invitation.

The attacker:

1. **Used stolen credentials** to access the employee's laptop remotely.
2. **Installed a keylogger** to steal login credentials for **internal systems**.
3. **Escalated privileges**, gaining **full control** over the company's cloud storage.

The Impact:

- **60GB of sensitive data** was **exfiltrated** and sold on the dark web.
- The company **suffered $15 million in damages**, including legal fees and lost business.
- **Security protocols were updated**, but **only after the damage was done**.

Lessons Learned:

✅ **Always enable MFA** – Even if passwords are stolen, MFA prevents unauthorized access.
✅ **Use EDR to detect intrusions** – A well-configured

EDR system would have **detected the keylogger**. ☑ **Train employees on phishing awareness** – Most cyber attacks begin with **a simple phishing email**.

Key Takeaways

✔ **Antivirus alone isn't enough** – Modern **EDR solutions provide real-time detection and response**.

✔ **Limiting user privileges** prevents malware from spreading across networks.

✔ **Application security and patch management** are critical to preventing endpoint vulnerabilities.

✔ **A single compromised laptop** can lead to a **multi-million dollar cyber attack**.

Next Chapter: Data Protection and Encryption

In **Chapter 8**, we'll dive into **how to protect sensitive data** with **encryption, secure storage, and backup strategies**.

🔒 Your data is valuable—let's make sure hackers never get their hands on it! 🚀

CHAPTER 8

Data Protection and Encryption

Introduction

Data is one of the most valuable assets in the digital world. Whether it's personal information, financial records, intellectual property, or government secrets, **keeping data secure** is crucial. However, cybercriminals are always looking for ways to **steal, alter, or exploit** sensitive data.

One of the most powerful tools for protecting data is **encryption**—a method that transforms data into an unreadable format unless the correct key is used. Encryption ensures that even if hackers gain access to sensitive data, they **cannot use or understand it**.

In this chapter, we'll explore:

- **Why encryption matters** – The importance of encrypting data at rest and in transit.
- **How to use encryption effectively** – Understanding AES, RSA, TLS/SSL.
- **The risks of weak encryption** – Real-world breaches caused by poor encryption practices.

By the end of this chapter, you'll know **how to protect sensitive data using strong encryption techniques**.

---

1. Why Encryption Matters: Data at Rest and Data in Transit

Encryption is used to protect data in **two main states**:

1. **Data at Rest** – Data that is stored (on hard drives, databases, cloud storage, USB drives).
2. **Data in Transit** – Data that is being transferred (between users, networks, cloud services).

A. Data at Rest: Protecting Stored Information

Data stored on a device or cloud service is vulnerable to:

- **Insider threats** – Employees or contractors accessing data without permission.
- **Theft of physical devices** – Stolen laptops, hard drives, or USB drives.
- **Hacker intrusions** – Cybercriminals breaching databases or cloud storage.

✅ Best Practices for Encrypting Data at Rest:

- Use **Full Disk Encryption (FDE)** for hard drives (BitLocker, FileVault).
- Encrypt **databases** and **backups** to prevent unauthorized access.
- Store encryption **keys separately** from the encrypted data.

📌 **Real-World Example:**
In **2014, an unencrypted laptop** stolen from a **hospital** led to the exposure of **4.5 million patient records**. **Lesson: Encrypting stored data prevents unauthorized access in case of theft.**

B. Data in Transit: Securing Communication Channels

Data that is being transferred over networks is vulnerable to:

- **Man-in-the-Middle (MitM) attacks** – Hackers intercepting and modifying communications.
- **Packet sniffing** – Attackers capturing data packets over public Wi-Fi.
- **Session hijacking** – Attackers stealing login sessions on insecure networks.

☑️ **Best Practices for Encrypting Data in Transit:**

- Use **TLS/SSL encryption** for websites and online services.
- Encrypt **email communications** using **PGP** or **S/MIME**.
- Always use **secure VPNs** when accessing sensitive data remotely.

📌 **Real-World Example:**
In **2018, hackers intercepted unencrypted emails** sent between **bank employees** and **stole $60 million** through fake wire transfers.
Lesson: Unencrypted data in transit can be easily intercepted—always use strong encryption protocols.

---

2. How to Use Encryption Effectively: AES, RSA, TLS/SSL

There are multiple encryption algorithms, each suited for different use cases. The most commonly used encryption standards are **AES**, **RSA**, and **TLS/SSL**.

A. AES (Advanced Encryption Standard) – The Gold Standard for Data Encryption

AES (Advanced Encryption Standard) is the most widely used encryption algorithm for protecting **stored data**.

How AES Works:

- Uses a **symmetric encryption** method (same key for encryption and decryption).
- Available in **128-bit, 192-bit, and 256-bit** key sizes (**AES-256 is the strongest**).
- Used by **banks, governments, and cloud storage services**.

☑ **Where AES is Used:**

- **Full Disk Encryption** (BitLocker, FileVault).
- **Encrypted databases** (MySQL, PostgreSQL).
- **Secure messaging apps** (WhatsApp, Signal).

📌 **Real-World Example:** The U.S. National Security Agency (NSA) has approved **AES-256** encryption for **top-secret government communications**.

Lesson: AES encryption is one of the most secure ways to protect data at rest.

B. RSA (Rivest-Shamir-Adleman) – Secure Key Exchange

RSA encryption is commonly used for **secure data transmission** and digital signatures.

How RSA Works:

- Uses **asymmetric encryption** (a **public key** for encryption and a **private key** for decryption).
- Slower than AES but **ideal for securing online transactions**.
- Used in **SSL/TLS encryption, email encryption**, and **digital signatures**.

✅ **Where RSA is Used:**

- **Secure websites** (HTTPS connections).
- **Email encryption** (PGP, S/MIME).
- **Cryptographic authentication** (SSH keys, digital signatures).

📌 **Real-World Example:**
In **2010, a weakness was discovered in RSA's encryption keys**, allowing hackers to break into **government and corporate networks**.
Lesson: **RSA keys should be at least 2048-bits for strong security.**

C. TLS/SSL – Encrypting Online Communications

TLS (Transport Layer Security) and **SSL (Secure Sockets Layer)** encrypt **data in transit**, ensuring secure web browsing and online transactions.

How TLS/SSL Works:

- Uses **both AES and RSA encryption** for secure communication.
- Protects against **MitM attacks and eavesdropping**.
- Displayed as a **padlock icon (🔒) in web browsers** when visiting secure websites.

✅ **Where TLS/SSL is Used:**

- **E-commerce websites** (protecting credit card payments).
- **Email servers** (securing email transmissions).
- **VPN connections** (encrypting remote access).

📌   **Real-World**   **Example:** In **2014, the Heartbleed vulnerability** in **OpenSSL** exposed sensitive data from **millions of websites**. **Lesson: TLS encryption should always be updated to the latest version to prevent vulnerabilities.**

---

3. The Risks of Weak Encryption: Real-World Breaches

Even when encryption is used, **weak encryption methods** can still lead to security breaches. Let's examine **three major encryption failures** and what went wrong.

A. The LinkedIn Password Breach (2012)

- **What**   **happened?** LinkedIn stored user passwords using **weak SHA-1 encryption**, making them **easy to crack**.
- **Impact:** Over **117 million user passwords** were leaked and sold on the dark web.

- **Lesson:**
  Use **strong hashing algorithms** like **bcrypt, Argon2, or PBKDF2** for storing passwords.

B. The Marriott Hotel Data Breach (2018)

- **What   happened?**
  Hackers stole **500 million customer records**, including passport and payment card data.
- **Impact:**
  Weak encryption keys allowed attackers to decrypt **customer data easily**.
- **Lesson:**
  Encryption is useless if keys are not properly protected—use **HSM (Hardware Security Modules)** for key management.

C. The Sony PlayStation Hack (2011)

- **What   happened?**
  Sony stored sensitive customer data **without encryption**, exposing **77 million accounts**.
- **Impact:**
  Hackers stole **credit card numbers, passwords, and addresses**.
- **Lesson:**
  All sensitive data must be encrypted at rest and in transit.

Key Takeaways

✔ **Encryption is essential for protecting sensitive data at rest and in transit.**
✔ **AES-256, RSA-2048, and TLS/SSL are industry-standard encryption methods.**
✔ **Weak encryption or poor key management can lead to massive data breaches.**
✔ **Encryption must be combined with strong authentication and access controls.**

Next Chapter: Cloud Security – Protecting Your Data in the Cloud

In **Chapter 9**, we'll explore **how to secure cloud storage**, prevent **cloud misconfigurations**, and protect data from **unauthorized access**.

🔒 **Encryption is only one piece of the puzzle—let's secure the cloud next!** 🚀

CHAPTER 9

Cloud Security – Protecting Your Data in the Cloud

Introduction

As organizations **migrate to the cloud**, securing data and applications has become a **top priority**. Cloud computing offers **scalability, flexibility, and cost savings**, but it also introduces new security challenges. **Data breaches, misconfigurations, and unauthorized access** are major risks if cloud security is not properly managed.

This chapter will cover:

- **The Cloud Security Shared Responsibility Model** – Who is responsible for securing what?
- **How to Secure AWS, Azure, and Google Cloud** – Best practices for protecting cloud environments.
- **Case Study: A Cloud Misconfiguration That Exposed Millions of Records** – How one mistake led to a massive data leak.

By the end of this chapter, you'll understand how to **secure your cloud assets, avoid common pitfalls, and protect sensitive data from cyber threats**.

---

1. The Cloud Security Shared Responsibility Model

Many organizations assume that **cloud providers handle all security**—this is **a dangerous misconception**. The **Shared**

Responsibility Model outlines which security aspects **cloud providers** manage and which are the responsibility of the **customer**.

A. Who Is Responsible for What?

Security Component	Cloud Provider Responsibility	Customer Responsibility
Data Protection	Provides **encryption options** and **access controls**.	Encrypts sensitive data and **manages access permissions**.
Operating System Security	Manages infrastructure security and patches.	Configures firewalls and **keeps software updated**.
Network Security	Protects **global cloud infrastructure**.	Sets up **virtual networks, security groups, and VPNs**.
Identity & Access Management (IAM)	Provides authentication and logging tools.	Manages **user permissions and access policies**.
Application Security	Ensures secure APIs and platform updates.	Secures **apps, databases, and third-party integrations**.

B. Common Security Mistakes in Cloud Environments

1. **Misconfigured Storage Buckets** – Exposing sensitive data publicly.

2. **Weak IAM Policies** – Granting excessive permissions to users and apps.
3. **Unpatched Cloud Workloads** – Leaving virtual machines vulnerable.
4. **No Logging or Monitoring** – Missing critical security alerts.

✅ **Key Takeaway: Cloud providers secure the infrastructure, but customers must secure their own applications and data.**

---

2. Securing AWS, Azure, and Google Cloud Environments

Each cloud provider (AWS, Azure, Google Cloud) offers **security tools and best practices** to protect cloud resources. Below are key security strategies for **each platform**.

A. Securing Amazon Web Services (AWS)

AWS is the **largest cloud provider**, used by **millions of organizations** worldwide. While AWS provides security tools, **customers must properly configure them** to avoid risks.

AWS Security Best Practices:

✅ **Use IAM Roles and Policies** – Follow **least privilege access** (only grant users the permissions they need).
✅ **Enable Multi-Factor Authentication (MFA)** – Protects AWS root accounts and admin users.
✅ **Encrypt S3 Buckets** – Prevents **unauthorized access** to stored data.

✅ **Enable AWS CloudTrail** – Monitors and logs account activity.

✅ **Use AWS Security Groups** – Restricts access to **EC2 instances** and databases.

📌 **Real-World Example:** In **2019, Capital One suffered a data breach** when **a misconfigured AWS S3 bucket** exposed **100 million customer records**. **Lesson: Always enable encryption and restrict access to cloud storage.**

B. Securing Microsoft Azure

Microsoft Azure is widely used by **enterprises and government organizations**. It offers **built-in security tools**, but customers must **properly configure** them.

Azure Security Best Practices:

✅ **Enable Azure Security Center** – Provides **threat detection and security recommendations**.

✅ **Use Azure AD Conditional Access** – Restricts access based on **user location and device health**.

✅ **Implement Network Security Groups (NSGs)** – Controls **inbound and outbound traffic**.

✅ **Encrypt Virtual Machines (VMs)** – Prevents attackers from accessing cloud-hosted data.

✅ **Use Azure Key Vault** – Securely stores **encryption keys and secrets**.

📌 **Real-World Example:** In **2021, a misconfigured Azure database exposed 38 million sensitive records**, including **COVID-19 testing details and government employee data**. **Lesson: Use strong access controls and audit cloud configurations regularly.**

C. Securing Google Cloud Platform (GCP)

Google Cloud is popular for **AI, analytics, and enterprise applications**. Like AWS and Azure, **GCP security depends on proper configuration**.

GCP Security Best Practices:

☑ **Use Google IAM Policies** – Restrict permissions to **only authorized users**.
☑ **Enable VPC Firewall Rules** – Blocks **unauthorized network traffic**.
☑ **Use Cloud Identity-Aware Proxy (IAP)** – Protects cloud applications from direct internet access.
☑ **Enable Cloud Logging & Monitoring** – Detects and responds to security threats.
☑ **Encrypt Cloud Storage Data** – Uses **Google-managed encryption keys** or **customer-managed keys**.

📌 **Real-World Example:** In **2018, Google Cloud services suffered an outage** after a **misconfigured firewall rule** blocked **legitimate traffic**. **Lesson: Carefully review firewall and access control settings** before deploying cloud applications.

94

3. Case Study: A Cloud Misconfiguration That Exposed Millions of Records

Case Study: The Facebook Data Leak (2021)

What Happened?

In **April 2021**, security researchers discovered **533 million Facebook user records** exposed **on an unprotected cloud server**. The leaked data included:

- **Phone numbers**
- **Full names**
- **Email addresses**
- **Location details**

How the Breach Happened:

1. **Facebook stored user data in a third-party cloud database**.
2. **The database was misconfigured**, leaving it **publicly accessible** without authentication.
3. **Hackers scraped the data and sold it on the dark web**.

Impact of the Breach:

- **Millions of Facebook users' data was exposed**, leading to **phishing attacks and identity theft**.
- **Regulatory scrutiny increased**, with **GDPR fines and lawsuits** filed against Facebook.

Lessons Learned:

☑ **Always restrict cloud storage access** – Set **S3 buckets, Azure Blobs, and Google Cloud Storage to private**.
☑ **Monitor cloud activity** – Use **AWS CloudTrail, Azure Monitor, and GCP Logging**.
☑ **Encrypt sensitive cloud data** – Even if data is leaked, encryption **prevents hackers from reading it**.

Key Takeaways

✔ **Cloud security follows a shared responsibility model** – Cloud providers protect the infrastructure, but **customers must secure their own data**.
✔ **Misconfigurations are the #1 cause of cloud breaches** – Always review **storage permissions, IAM policies, and network settings**.
✔ **AWS, Azure, and Google Cloud offer powerful security tools** – But they must be **properly configured** to be effective.
✔ **The Facebook data leak highlights the dangers of poor cloud security** – Always **encrypt sensitive data and restrict access**.

Next Chapter: Penetration Testing – Thinking Like an Attacker

In **Chapter 10**, we'll explore **penetration testing**, including how ethical hackers **find vulnerabilities, exploit misconfigurations, and test security defenses**.

🔍 To defend against hackers, you must think like one. Let's learn how penetration testing works! 🚀

CHAPTER 10

Penetration Testing – Thinking Like an Attacker

Introduction

The best way to defend against cyber threats is to **think like an attacker**. **Penetration testing (pen testing)** is the practice of simulating real-world attacks to identify and fix security vulnerabilities **before hackers exploit them**.

In this chapter, we will explore:

- **What penetration testing is and why it's important**
- **The five phases of a penetration test**
- **Essential ethical hacking tools: Kali Linux, Metasploit, and Nmap**

By the end of this chapter, you'll understand how penetration testing helps organizations **strengthen their defenses** and **stay ahead of cybercriminals**.

1. What is Penetration Testing and Why is it Important?

Penetration testing is a **controlled cyber attack** where security professionals (ethical hackers) attempt to **find vulnerabilities in systems, networks, and applications** before malicious hackers do.

Penetration tests help organizations:
☑ Identify **security weaknesses** in applications, networks,

and   devices.

☑ Validate **existing security controls** to see if they can withstand   real   attacks.

☑ Meet **compliance requirements** (e.g., PCI-DSS, GDPR,   ISO   27001).

☑ Reduce the risk of **data breaches and financial losses**.

A. Different Types of Penetration Tests

Penetration Test Type	Description	Example
Network Penetration Testing	Identifies vulnerabilities in an organization's internal and external networks.	Testing firewalls, VPNs, and network segmentation.
Web Application Penetration Testing	Focuses on **web applications and APIs**, looking for security flaws.	Detecting SQL injection, cross-site scripting (XSS), and authentication issues.
Wireless Penetration Testing	Examines the security of **Wi-Fi networks** and their encryption.	Testing for **WPA2/WPA3 vulnerabilities and rogue access points**.
Physical Penetration Testing	Tests **physical security** like locked doors, access cards, and surveillance systems.	Gaining **unauthorized access** to a data center.

Penetration Test Type	Description	Example
Social Engineering Penetration Testing	Simulates **phishing, phone scams, and in-person deception** to test employee awareness.	Sending fake emails to test if employees click on malicious links.

📌 **Real-World Example:** In **2017, security researchers hired by a bank** conducted a **social engineering penetration test**. They **gained physical access to a data center** by dressing as IT support, then **plugged a USB device into a server** to deploy malware. **Lesson: Cybersecurity isn't just about firewalls—human weaknesses can be the biggest vulnerability.**

2. The Five Phases of a Penetration Test

A penetration test follows a **structured methodology** to simulate real attacks while maintaining **ethical and legal boundaries**.

Phase 1: Reconnaissance (Information Gathering)

The first step is **gathering information about the target** to identify weak points before launching an attack.

✅ Types of Reconnaissance:

- **Passive Reconnaissance** – Gathering publicly available information (OSINT, social media, WHOIS records).

- **Active Reconnaissance** – Actively probing systems (e.g., scanning for open ports with Nmap).

🛠 Tools Used:

- **Google Dorking** – Using Google search to find exposed files and login pages.
- **Shodan** – A search engine for **internet-connected devices** (e.g., routers, cameras, IoT).
- **WHOIS Lookup** – Reveals domain name registration details.

Phase 2: Scanning (Identifying Vulnerabilities)

Once reconnaissance is complete, the penetration tester **scans the target network for open ports, running services, and vulnerabilities**.

✅ Common Scanning Techniques:

- **Port Scanning** – Identifies which ports are open (Nmap, Masscan).
- **Vulnerability Scanning** – Finds security flaws in services and software (Nessus, OpenVAS).
- **Banner Grabbing** – Extracts information about running services (e.g., Apache, MySQL versions).

🛠 Tools Used:

- **Nmap** – Maps the network and finds open ports.
- **Nessus** – Detects known vulnerabilities in systems.
- **Nikto** – Scans for **web server vulnerabilities**.

Phase 3: Exploitation (Gaining Access)

The penetration tester **attempts to exploit** vulnerabilities discovered in the previous phases. This is where ethical hackers **simulate real cyber attacks** to test defenses.

✅ Common Exploitation Techniques:

- **Brute Force Attacks** – Guessing weak passwords using automated tools.
- **SQL Injection** – Extracting sensitive data from a database via a web app.
- **Remote Code Execution (RCE)** – Gaining control over a system through vulnerable software.

⚒ Tools Used:

- **Metasploit** – A powerful exploitation framework for testing vulnerabilities.
- **SQLmap** – Automated SQL injection testing tool.
- **Hydra** – Brute-force attack tool for guessing passwords.

📌   **Real-World**   **Example:**
In **2015, hackers used an SQL injection exploit** to breach **TalkTalk, a UK telecom company**, stealing **156,000 customer   records**.
Lesson: Web applications should always validate and sanitize user input.

Phase 4: Post-Exploitation (Maintaining Access & Data Exfiltration)

Once access is gained, ethical hackers simulate **how an attacker would maintain control** and **extract sensitive data**.

✅ Common Post-Exploitation Actions:

- **Privilege Escalation** – Gaining higher-level access (e.g., from a user account to admin).
- **Lateral Movement** – Expanding access across an organization's network.
- **Data Exfiltration** – Extracting sensitive data like credit card details or intellectual property.

🛠 Tools Used:

- **Mimikatz** – Extracts Windows credentials from memory.
- **BloodHound** – Maps Active Directory vulnerabilities.

Phase 5: Reporting & Remediation

The final phase involves **documenting findings and recommending fixes**.

✅ Penetration Test Report Includes:

- **Vulnerabilities found and exploited.**
- **Risk assessment and impact analysis.**
- **Steps for remediation and improving security posture.**

📌 **Real-World Example:**
In **2020, a penetration test uncovered an unpatched vulnerability** in a **hospital's network,** which could have allowed **attackers to shut down life-saving medical equipment**.

Lesson: Penetration testing saves lives and protects critical infrastructure.

---

3. Ethical Hacking Tools: Kali Linux, Metasploit, Nmap

Ethical hackers use specialized tools to conduct penetration tests legally and effectively.

A. Kali Linux: The Ethical Hacker's OS

Kali Linux is a **penetration testing operating system** preloaded with hundreds of security tools.

✅ Key Kali Linux Tools:

- **Nmap** – Network scanning.
- **Metasploit** – Exploitation framework.
- **Burp Suite** – Web application security testing.
- **John the Ripper** – Password cracking.

📌 Why Kali Linux?

- Used by **cybersecurity professionals and ethical hackers worldwide**.
- Free and open-source.

B. Metasploit: The Ultimate Exploitation Framework

Metasploit is an **offensive security tool** that helps ethical hackers find and exploit vulnerabilities.

✅ What Metasploit Can Do:

- Scan for vulnerabilities.
- Exploit security weaknesses.
- Create custom payloads for penetration tests.

📌 **Metasploit in Action:** A penetration tester **used Metasploit to exploit an unpatched server**, gaining **full admin access** to a company's database.

Lesson: Regular software updates are critical to stopping hackers.

C. Nmap: The Network Mapper

Nmap (Network Mapper) is a **powerful tool for discovering devices and scanning open ports**.

✅ What Nmap Can Do:

- Detect open ports and running services.
- Identify firewall rules and network security gaps.
- Find outdated software versions.

📌 **Nmap in Action:** Hackers used **Nmap to scan for open Remote Desktop Protocol (RDP) ports**, targeting **organizations vulnerable to ransomware**.

Lesson: Disable unused services and restrict external access.

Key Takeaways

✔ **Penetration testing helps organizations identify and fix security weaknesses.**
✔ **The five phases of penetration testing** follow a structured attack methodology.
✔ **Ethical hacking tools (Kali Linux, Metasploit, Nmap) are essential for security professionals.**

Next Chapter: Social Engineering – The Art of Human Hacking

In **Chapter 11**, we'll explore **how attackers manipulate human behavior** through **phishing, pretexting, and other social engineering tactics**.

🐱 **Hackers don't just exploit computers—they exploit people. Let's dive in!** 🚀

CHAPTER 11

Social Engineering – The Art of Human Hacking

Introduction

The weakest link in cybersecurity isn't always **technology— it's people**. **Social engineering** is a psychological attack where hackers manipulate **human behavior** to trick individuals into **revealing sensitive information, clicking on malicious links, or granting unauthorized access**. Unlike technical hacking, social engineering **exploits human trust** rather than software vulnerabilities.

Why Social Engineering Works

✔ People are **naturally trusting** and want to be helpful.

✔ Attackers **exploit fear, urgency, and curiosity**.

✔ Many users lack **awareness** of cyber threats.

In this chapter, we will explore:

- **How attackers manipulate human behavior** – The psychology behind social engineering.
- **Real-world phishing scams and how to spot them** – Examples of common tactics.
- **How to protect employees and organizations from social engineering** – Strategies to defend against manipulation.

By the end of this chapter, you'll understand how **social engineers operate**, and how to **spot and prevent** these attacks before they succeed.

1. How Attackers Manipulate Human Behavior

Social engineers are **masters of deception**. They use psychological tricks to manipulate victims into **revealing passwords, transferring money, or installing malware**.

A. The Psychological Tactics of Social Engineering

Tactic	Description	Example
Authority	Impersonating a high-ranking official to demand action.	Fake CEO email asking for a wire transfer.
Urgency	Pressuring the victim to act quickly.	"Your account will be locked in 24 hours!"
Fear	Creating anxiety to force compliance.	"You've been hacked! Click here to fix it."
Greed	Offering financial rewards or fake prizes.	"Congratulations! You've won a $500 gift card."
Curiosity	Tricking users into clicking infected links.	"See who viewed your profile!"
Trust	Exploiting personal connections or familiar brands.	"This is IT support, we need your password."

✅ **Key Takeaway:** Social engineers **manipulate emotions and exploit trust** to trick their victims.

2. Real-World Phishing Scams and How to Spot Them

Phishing is the most common form of social engineering. It involves sending fraudulent emails, texts, or phone calls to **steal credentials, money, or sensitive data**.

A. Types of Phishing Attacks

Type of Phishing	How It Works	Example
Email Phishing	Fake emails trick victims into clicking malicious links.	A fake PayPal email asking for login credentials.
Spear Phishing	Targeted attacks on specific individuals or companies.	A hacker emails an executive pretending to be their assistant.
Whaling	High-level phishing attacks against CEOs or executives.	"This is your CFO, transfer $50,000 to this account now."
Vishing (Voice Phishing)	Fraudulent phone calls impersonating legitimate entities.	"This is the IRS, you owe taxes. Pay immediately!"
Smishing (SMS Phishing)	Fake text messages with malicious links.	"Your Amazon package delivery failed. Click here to reschedule."

Type of Phishing	How It Works	Example
Baiting	Luring victims with free offers or fake downloads.	"Download this free software update!"

📌 Real-World Example: The Google & Facebook Scam ($100 Million Fraud)

- A hacker impersonated a **trusted vendor** and sent fake invoices to Google and Facebook.
- Employees **approved the payments** without verifying the sender.
- Over **$100 million** was stolen before the scam was detected.

Lesson: Always verify financial transactions and email senders before taking action.

B. How to Spot a Phishing Attempt

☑ **Check the Sender's Email** – Does the sender's email match the legitimate domain? Example: **support@paypal.com** vs. **support@paypa1.com** (notice the number 1 instead of an "l").

☑ **Look for Urgency or Threats** – If an email demands "Immediate Action" or "Your Account Will Be Closed," be suspicious.

☑ **Hover Over Links** – Before clicking, hover over the link to see if it directs to a legitimate website.

☑ **Check for Grammar & Spelling Errors** – Many

phishing emails contain poor grammar and spelling mistakes.

✅ **Verify with the Company Directly** – Call the official support line instead of clicking on links.

📌 **Real-World Example: The Twitter Hack (2020)**

- Attackers used **spear phishing** to trick Twitter employees into revealing login credentials.
- The hackers gained access to **high-profile accounts**, including **Elon Musk and Barack Obama**.
- They posted fake cryptocurrency giveaways, scamming users out of **hundreds of thousands of dollars**.

Lesson: Employees should always verify unexpected login requests with IT departments before providing credentials.

3. Protecting Employees and Organizations from Social Engineering

Because social engineering **targets human behavior**, organizations must focus on **training employees and implementing security measures**.

A. Security Awareness Training

Organizations should conduct **regular security training** to teach employees how to recognize and report **phishing attempts, scams, and impersonation attacks**.

✅ **Best Practices for Security Training:**

- Use **realistic phishing simulations** to test employee awareness.
- Teach employees to **never share credentials over email or phone**.
- Encourage a **"Think Before You Click"** culture.
- Provide a **clear process** for reporting suspicious emails.

📌 **Real-World Example: How Security Training Prevented a $2 Million Fraud**
An employee at a **major law firm** received an email requesting a **large fund transfer**. However, because of **regular security training**, they called the CFO to verify the request.

💡 **Result:** The transfer was **fraudulent**, and **$2 million was saved**.

B. Implementing Technical Defenses Against Social Engineering

Technical controls help prevent social engineering attacks before they reach users.

✅ **Key Security Measures:**
◆ **Enable Multi-Factor Authentication (MFA)** – Even if credentials are stolen, attackers can't log in without MFA.
◆ **Use Email Filtering & Anti-Phishing Tools** – Blocks suspicious emails and malicious links.
◆ **Implement Least Privilege Access** – Prevents employees from accessing data they don't need.
◆ **Monitor Network Activity** – Detects unusual login attempts or account takeovers.
◆ **Restrict Use of Personal Emails for Work** – Reduces exposure to phishing risks.

📌 **Real-World Example: The Ubiquiti Email Scam (2021) – $46 Million Lost**

- Attackers **spoofed** an email from the company's CEO and **requested wire transfers**.
- Employees **approved** the transactions without verifying.
- The company **lost $46 million** before realizing it was a scam.

Lesson: Always verify financial transactions and use multi-person approval processes.

C. The Role of Red Team Testing

Red Team testing involves **ethical hackers simulating social engineering attacks** to evaluate how employees respond.

✅ **Common Red Team Exercises:**

- **Fake phishing emails** to see how many employees click links.
- **Pretexting tests** to evaluate employee awareness.
- **Impersonation attempts** (e.g., pretending to be IT support).

📌 **Real-World Example: A Red Team Social Engineering Test at a Tech Company**

- A Red Team **called employees pretending to be IT support**.
- **30% of employees provided their login credentials** over the phone.

- **Result:** The company **improved security training** and implemented strict identity verification.

Key Takeaways

✔ **Social engineering manipulates human behavior to bypass security measures.**
✔ **Phishing is the most common social engineering attack**, affecting both individuals and businesses.
✔ **Recognizing warning signs like urgency, authority, and poor grammar can prevent phishing.**
✔ **Security awareness training, technical defenses, and Red Team testing help organizations stay protected.**

Next Chapter: Red Team vs. Blue Team – Simulating Real Attacks

In **Chapter 12**, we'll dive into **how cybersecurity teams simulate attacks** to **test and improve security defenses**.

🖐 **Want to see how Red Teams attack and Blue Teams defend? Let's go!** 🚀

CHAPTER 12

Red Team vs. Blue Team – Simulating Real Attacks

Introduction

Cybersecurity is not just about **defensive measures**—it's about **actively testing and improving security**. Organizations use **Red Team vs. Blue Team exercises** to simulate **real-world cyberattacks** and strengthen their defenses. These simulations help uncover **security weaknesses** before **real hackers exploit them**.

In this chapter, we'll explore:

- **The difference between Red Teaming and Blue Teaming** – Offensive vs. defensive cybersecurity strategies.
- **How companies simulate real-world attacks to test defenses** – The Red Team's tactics and the Blue Team's countermeasures.
- **Case study: A Red Team assessment that exposed major security flaws** – How ethical hackers identified and fixed vulnerabilities.

By the end of this chapter, you'll understand **how cybersecurity teams operate during an attack simulation** and why these exercises are crucial for **improving an organization's security posture**.

1. The Difference Between Red Teaming and Blue Teaming

A. What is a Red Team? (Attackers)

A **Red Team** is a **group of ethical hackers** who act like real cybercriminals to **simulate attacks on an organization**. Their goal is to **find weaknesses before malicious hackers do**.

✅ **Red Team Objectives:**
✔ Identify **security gaps** in networks, applications, and physical security.
✔ **Bypass defenses** and gain unauthorized access.
✔ **Test employee awareness** with social engineering tactics.
✔ Demonstrate **real-world attack scenarios** to executives.

B. What is a Blue Team? (Defenders)

A **Blue Team** consists of **security professionals** who defend the organization against **Red Team attacks**. Their role is to **detect, analyze, and respond** to simulated cyber threats.

✅ **Blue Team Objectives:**
✔ Monitor **network traffic and system logs** for attack indicators.
✔ Strengthen **firewalls, endpoint security, and access controls**.
✔ Respond to attacks in **real-time** and investigate threats.
✔ Improve **incident response and security policies**.

C. Red Team vs. Blue Team: Key Differences

Feature	Red Team (Attackers)	Blue Team (Defenders)
Primary Goal	Simulate real-world cyberattacks	Detect and defend against attacks
Role	Offensive security (ethical hacking)	Defensive security (threat monitoring)
Techniques Used	Social engineering, penetration testing, malware deployment	Firewalls, intrusion detection, log analysis
Outcome	Identifies vulnerabilities	Strengthens security measures

📌 **Key Takeaway: Red Teams attack, Blue Teams defend, and together they improve cybersecurity resilience.**

---

2. How Companies Simulate Real-World Attacks to Test Defenses

Organizations conduct **Red Team vs. Blue Team exercises** to **evaluate their security readiness**. These tests **simulate real-world cyberattacks** without actually causing harm.

A. The Red Team Attack Simulation Process

1 **Reconnaissance (Information Gathering)** – The Red Team collects **OSINT (Open-Source Intelligence)** on employees, networks, and security controls.

2 **Initial Compromise** – The Red Team attempts to **bypass firewalls, exploit vulnerabilities, or use phishing attacks to gain access.**

3 **Privilege Escalation** – Once inside, they try to **gain higher-level access** (e.g., from a regular user to an administrator).

4 **Lateral Movement** – Attackers move across the network, looking for **sensitive data, servers, and backups.**

5 **Data Exfiltration** – The Red Team attempts to **steal simulated sensitive data** to show the risk of a real breach.

B. The Blue Team's Response Strategy

✅ **Threat Detection** – Monitors **network logs, endpoint activity, and user behavior** to spot Red Team activity.

✅ **Incident Response** – Blue Team analysts **identify the attack, isolate compromised systems, and neutralize threats**.

✅ **Security Hardening** – After the exercise, the Blue Team **patches vulnerabilities and strengthens defenses**.

📌 **Example: A Red Team successfully uses a phishing email to steal credentials. The Blue Team detects unauthorized logins and blocks access before data is stolen.**

---

3. Case Study: A Red Team Assessment That Exposed Major Security Flaws

Case Study: A Financial Institution's Weak Security Controls

Scenario:

A **large financial company** hired a Red Team to test its security. The goal was to **assess how vulnerable the company was to cyber threats**.

Red Team Attack Plan:

1 **Phishing Attack** – The Red Team sent a fake email posing as the company's IT department, asking employees to **reset their   passwords**.
2 **Credential Theft** – Several employees **fell for the scam** and provided their login details.
3 **Gaining Access** – Using stolen credentials, the Red Team **logged into internal systems** and **escalated privileges**.
4 **Lateral Movement** – They **moved through the network** undetected for **three days**, collecting sensitive customer data.
5 **Simulated Data Breach** – The Red Team successfully **exfiltrated fake financial records**, demonstrating a real-world attack scenario.

Blue Team's Response:

☑ **Detected suspicious logins from unrecognized locations.**
☑ **Blocked access and forced password resets.**
☑ **Implemented new email security rules to filter phishing   emails.**
☑ **Strengthened multi-factor authentication (MFA) to prevent unauthorized logins.**

Outcome & Lessons Learned

◆ The company **was not prepared for phishing attacks—** they launched mandatory **security awareness training**. ◆ **MFA was enforced** across all employee accounts. ◆ Security logs were **monitored in real-time** to detect unusual activity.

📌 **Key Takeaway: A well-executed Red Team exercise exposed weaknesses that could have led to a real cyberattack. The Blue Team used the findings to improve security.**

---

4. The Future: Purple Teaming & Continuous Security Testing

While Red and Blue Teams operate separately, some organizations use a **Purple Team approach**, where both teams **collaborate in real-time**.

A. What is Purple Teaming?

- Combines **Red Team's attack tactics** with **Blue Team's defense strategies**.
- Encourages **continuous learning and improvement**.
- Helps security teams **stay ahead of evolving threats**.

B. How Companies Can Implement Continuous Security Testing

✅ **Run Red Team simulations regularly** to uncover weaknesses.

☑ **Conduct Blue Team defense drills** to improve detection and response.

☑ **Use automated security tools** for **real-time threat detection**.

☑ **Adopt a Purple Team approach** to enhance **team collaboration**.

📌 **Real-World Example:** A **tech company adopted a Purple Team approach**, where Red and Blue Teams **shared insights immediately**. As a result, they **reduced incident response times from 24 hours to under 2 hours**.

Lesson: Collaboration between attack and defense teams leads to better security outcomes.

Key Takeaways

✔ **Red Teams simulate real-world cyberattacks to identify vulnerabilities.**

✔ **Blue Teams defend against attacks and improve security measures.**

✔ **Red Team vs. Blue Team exercises help organizations strengthen security posture.**

✔ **A financial company's Red Team test revealed major flaws, leading to improved defenses.**

✔ **Purple Teaming fosters collaboration between attackers and defenders for continuous security improvement.**

Next Chapter: Threat Intelligence – Predicting and Preventing Attacks

In **Chapter 13**, we'll explore how **organizations use threat intelligence to track cybercriminals, predict attacks, and strengthen security defenses**.

🏯 **Want to predict cyber threats before they happen? Let's dive into threat intelligence next!** 🚀

CHAPTER 13

Securing Businesses and Organizations

Introduction

Cybersecurity is **no longer just an IT concern**—it's a **business priority**. Organizations of all sizes are **prime targets for cybercriminals**, and a single security breach can result in **financial loss, reputational damage, and regulatory fines**.

To build a strong cybersecurity posture, businesses must implement:

✔ **Comprehensive security policies and frameworks** to guide   employees.

✔ **Employee training programs** to prevent human errors.

✔ **Real-world case studies** to learn from past cybersecurity failures.

In this chapter, we will explore:

- **Cybersecurity policies and frameworks** – The foundation of secure business operations.
- **Employee awareness and training programs** – Why security culture is critical.
- **Real-world business cybersecurity failures** – What companies can learn from past mistakes.

By the end of this chapter, you'll understand how businesses can **effectively defend against cyber threats** and **build a security-first culture**.

1. Cybersecurity Policies and Frameworks

A **cybersecurity policy** is a set of **guidelines, rules, and best practices** that organizations implement to protect their digital assets. Without a strong policy, employees may **unknowingly put sensitive data at risk**.

A. Why Cybersecurity Policies Are Important

☑ **Standardizes security practices** across the organization.

☑ **Reduces the risk of human error** leading to data breaches.

☑ **Ensures compliance** with regulatory requirements (e.g., GDPR, ISO 27001).

☑ **Improves incident response** when cyberattacks occur.

B. Key Elements of a Strong Cybersecurity Policy

Policy Area	Purpose
Access Control Policy	Limits access to sensitive data using role-based permissions (least privilege).
Password Policy	Enforces **strong, unique passwords** and **multi-factor authentication (MFA)**.
Email and Communication Security	Prevents **phishing and social engineering** attacks by training employees.

Policy Area	Purpose
Incident Response Plan	Outlines **steps for detecting, responding to, and recovering from** cyber incidents.
Remote Work Security Policy	Defines security measures for **employees working remotely** (VPN, secure Wi-Fi, device encryption).
Data Retention & Encryption Policy	Ensures that sensitive data is **properly encrypted and securely stored**.
Third-Party Vendor Security	Verifies that **suppliers and partners follow security best practices**.

🔑 **Key Takeaway:** Cybersecurity policies must be **clear, enforced, and regularly updated** to keep up with **evolving threats**.

C. Cybersecurity Frameworks: Industry Best Practices

Organizations **don't need to start from scratch**—they can adopt **existing security frameworks**.

☑ **Popular Cybersecurity Frameworks:**

Framework	Purpose
NIST Cybersecurity Framework (CSF)	Provides a **risk-based approach** to managing cybersecurity threats.
ISO 27001	A globally recognized **standard for information security management**.
CIS Controls	Lists **security best practices** to prevent cyberattacks.
GDPR (General Data Protection Regulation)	Protects **personal data and privacy** for businesses operating in the EU.
SOC 2 Compliance	Ensures **secure handling of customer data** for service providers.

📌 **Example:** A financial institution implemented **ISO 27001** and **CIS Controls** to **protect customer banking data**. As a result, they reduced **fraud attempts by 40%** over two years.

Lesson: Adopting a cybersecurity framework helps businesses stay proactive and secure.

---

2. Employee Awareness and Training Programs

Even with **strong policies**, cybersecurity **only works if employees follow the rules**. Many breaches occur because employees **fall for phishing scams, use weak passwords, or mishandle sensitive data**.

126

A. Why Employee Cybersecurity Training is Essential

🪨 **85% of cyberattacks** involve **human error**—employees clicking on malicious links, falling for scams, or misconfiguring security settings.
📌 **Example:** The **Twitter hack (2020)** happened because employees fell for **social engineering attacks**, giving hackers access to high-profile accounts.

B. What an Effective Cybersecurity Training Program Includes

Training Focus	Why It Matters
Phishing Awareness	Educates employees on **spotting and reporting phishing emails**.
Password Security & MFA	Reinforces the use of **strong passwords** and **multi-factor authentication**.
Secure Remote Work Practices	Covers **VPN use, Wi-Fi security, and endpoint protection**.
Incident Reporting Procedures	Ensures employees **know how to report security incidents** quickly.
Handling Sensitive Data	Teaches best practices for **storing and sharing confidential information**.

☑ **Best Practices for Employee Training:** ✔ Conduct **regular phishing simulations** to test awareness.
✔ Provide **interactive training modules** instead of just

lectures.

✔ Offer **rewards for security-conscious behavior**.

📌 **Example:**
A tech company implemented **quarterly phishing simulations**. Before training, **40% of employees clicked on phishing emails**. After six months, the rate dropped to **less than 5%**.

Lesson: Cybersecurity training significantly reduces human error and security risks.

---

3. Real-World Business Cybersecurity Failures and Lessons Learned

Many organizations **ignore security risks** until it's too late. Let's examine **three major cybersecurity failures** and what businesses can learn from them.

A. Target Data Breach (2013)

What Happened?

- Attackers **gained access through a third-party HVAC vendor**.
- They **moved laterally through the network**, stealing **40 million credit card records**.

Lessons Learned:

✔ **Secure third-party access** – Vendors should have **limited access** to internal systems.

✔ **Monitor network activity** – Detect **unusual access patterns** in real-time.

B. Equifax Data Breach (2017)

What Happened?

- Hackers exploited an **unpatched software vulnerability** in **Apache Struts**.
- **147 million customers'** personal data was stolen.

Lessons Learned:

✔ **Patch software vulnerabilities quickly** – The exploit was known for **two months** before the breach.
✔ **Encrypt sensitive customer data** – Even if attackers break in, **encrypted data is useless**.

C. Maersk Ransomware Attack (2017)

What Happened?

- The **NotPetya ransomware** shut down **global shipping operations**, costing **$300 million**.
- Attackers **entered through a single unpatched server**.

Lessons Learned:

✔ **Implement strong endpoint security** – Block ransomware before it spreads.

✔️ **Have a disaster recovery plan** – Maersk had to **rebuild 4,000 servers** from backups.

📌 **Key Takeaway: Neglecting cybersecurity leads to major financial and operational damage.**

---

4. How Businesses Can Strengthen Their Cybersecurity

Cybersecurity is not a one-time task—it requires ongoing improvement.

✅ Steps Businesses Can Take Today:

✔️ **Adopt a cybersecurity framework** (NIST, ISO 27001, CIS Controls).

✔️ **Train employees regularly** on phishing, password security, and social engineering.

✔️ **Enable multi-factor authentication (MFA)** for all employee accounts.

✔️ **Implement strong access control policies** (least privilege).

✔️ **Monitor network activity** for suspicious behavior.

✔️ **Patch and update software regularly** to prevent exploits.

✔️ **Backup critical data** to recover from cyberattacks.

📌 **Example:**
A healthcare provider **implemented cybersecurity training, strong encryption, and 24/7 monitoring**. Over three years, **phishing attacks dropped by 90%**, and **data breaches were completely prevented**.

130

Lesson: Proactive cybersecurity measures prevent real-world disasters.

Key Takeaways

✔ **Cybersecurity policies and frameworks** provide structure for protecting businesses.
✔ **Employee training is critical** to prevent phishing, social engineering, and insider threats.
✔ **Real-world security failures (Target, Equifax, Maersk)** show the cost of weak security.
✔ **Businesses must continuously improve security** by adopting frameworks, training staff, and monitoring threats.

Next Chapter: Incident Response – What to Do When You're Hacked

In **Chapter 14**, we'll explore how companies **respond to cyberattacks, recover from breaches, and minimize damage**.

🪣 **A cyberattack is inevitable—let's learn how to respond effectively!** 🚀

CHAPTER 14

Incident Response – What to Do When You're Hacked

Introduction

Despite the best security measures, **cyber incidents are inevitable**. The key to minimizing damage is having a **well-prepared Incident Response (IR) plan**. Organizations that respond **quickly and effectively** to cyberattacks can **contain threats, reduce downtime, and prevent data loss**.

Why Incident Response Matters

✔ **Reduces financial and reputational damage** – A slow response increases **costs and legal consequences**.
✔ **Minimizes business disruption** – Downtime due to cyberattacks can be **crippling**.
✔ **Ensures compliance** – Many industries require businesses to **report and respond to data breaches**.

In this chapter, we will cover:

- **The Incident Response Lifecycle** – A structured approach to managing cyber incidents.
- **Real-world response strategies** – How to handle **ransomware, phishing, and insider threats**.
- **Case study: A company's real-time response to a data breach** – Lessons from a real cyberattack.

By the end of this chapter, you'll understand how businesses can **effectively detect, contain, and recover from cyberattacks**.

132

1. The Incident Response Lifecycle: The Five Phases

The **Incident Response Lifecycle**, as outlined by **NIST (National Institute of Standards and Technology)**, consists of **five critical phases**:

Phase	Objective	Key Actions
1. Preparation	Develop response plans, tools, and training.	Create **incident response teams**, run simulations.
2. Detection & Analysis	Identify and assess potential security incidents.	Use **SIEM tools, threat monitoring, and log analysis**.
3. Containment	Prevent the attack from spreading.	Isolate infected systems, disable compromised accounts.
4. Eradication & Recovery	Remove the threat and restore affected systems.	Clean malware, patch vulnerabilities, restore backups.
5. Post-Incident Review	Learn from the attack to improve future response.	Conduct **root cause analysis**, update security policies.

🔖 **Key Takeaway: A well-executed Incident Response plan helps minimize damage and strengthens security for future incidents.**

2. Real-World Response Strategies for Cyber Threats

A. Responding to a Ransomware Attack

◆ **Scenario:** A company discovers that **all files have been encrypted**, and hackers are demanding **Bitcoin payment** to restore access.

✅ **Immediate Response Steps:** 1 **Isolate infected systems** – Disconnect affected computers from the network to prevent spread.
2 **Determine the ransomware variant** – Some ransomware strains have **known decryption tools.**
3 **Notify the Incident Response Team (IRT)** – Activate the response plan.
4 **Restore from backups (if available)** – Avoid paying ransom if data can be recovered.
5 **Investigate entry points** – Identify how the ransomware got in (e.g., phishing email, RDP exploit).

📌 **Example: The Colonial Pipeline Ransomware Attack (2021)**

- Attackers used **a single compromised VPN password** to deploy ransomware.
- **Critical fuel supply** across the U.S. East Coast was disrupted for days.
- The company **paid a $4.4 million ransom**, but operations still suffered.

Lesson: Strong password policies, network segmentation, and offline backups could have prevented the disaster.

B. Responding to a Phishing Attack

◆ **Scenario:** An employee receives an email from "IT Support" asking them to **reset their password**. They click the link and enter credentials into a **fake login page**.

✅ **Immediate Response Steps:** 1 **Reset compromised accounts** – Force password changes for affected users. 2 **Investigate email headers** – Trace the phishing email's source.
3 **Block malicious domains** – Update email filters to prevent future attacks.
4 **Monitor for unauthorized logins** – Check for **suspicious access** to corporate accounts.
5 **Conduct phishing awareness training** – Educate employees to spot scams.

📌 **Example: The Twitter Phishing Hack (2020)**

- Attackers **tricked employees into revealing credentials**, giving them control over **high-profile Twitter accounts** (Elon Musk, Apple, Barack Obama).
- They posted **fraudulent Bitcoin scam tweets**, stealing **thousands of dollars**.
- **Lesson: Multi-Factor Authentication (MFA)** and **employee training** could have stopped the attack.

C. Responding to an Insider Threat

◆ **Scenario:** A disgruntled employee **copies confidential company data** onto a USB drive before leaving the company.

☑ **Immediate Response Steps:** 1 **Revoke access immediately** – Disable **ex-employee accounts** upon resignation.
2 **Monitor suspicious file transfers** – Check **USB usage logs and cloud storage activity**.
3 **Legal action if necessary** – If sensitive data is stolen, involve **legal and HR teams**.
4 **Implement Data Loss Prevention (DLP)** – Block unauthorized **file transfers and external devices**.
5 **Conduct exit interviews and security briefings** – Ensure employees **understand legal consequences** of data theft.

📌 **Example: Tesla Insider Threat (2020)**

- A **Tesla employee was bribed** by hackers to **install malware** on the company's network.
- The employee **reported the incident**, allowing Tesla to **prevent a major cyberattack**.
- **Lesson: Insider threat monitoring and employee reporting mechanisms** are critical for security.

---

3. Case Study: A Company's Real-Time Response to a Data Breach

Case Study: Marriott International Data Breach (2018)

What Happened?

- Hackers **gained access to Starwood Hotels' database** and stole **500 million customer records**.
- The breach **went undetected for four years** before discovery.

- Exposed data included **passport numbers, payment details, and personal information**.

Marriott's Incident Response Plan:

1 Detection & Investigation:

- Security teams **identified unusual database activity** and launched an investigation.
  ## 2 Containment:
- Marriott **disabled unauthorized access** and **monitored further intrusion attempts**.
  ## 3 Eradication & Recovery:
- Patching vulnerabilities and **enhancing network segmentation**.
  ## 4 Public Disclosure & Legal Response:
- **Notified affected customers** and cooperated with regulators.
- Paid **fines under GDPR** for failing to secure personal data.
  ## 5 Post-Incident Review:
- Strengthened **encryption and access controls**.
- Implemented **real-time threat monitoring** across all databases.

📌 **Key Takeaways:** ✔ **Regular security audits** could have detected the breach **much earlier**. ✔ **Encryption of sensitive customer data** would have minimized damage. ✔ **Proactive threat monitoring** is essential to **catch attackers before they cause damage**.

4. How to Build an Effective Incident Response Plan

☑ Steps to Improve Incident Response Readiness

✔ **Establish an Incident Response Team (IRT)** – Clearly define **roles** **and** **responsibilities**.

✔ **Develop a formal IR policy** – Follow **NIST or ISO 27035** **frameworks**.

✔ **Conduct regular security drills** – Simulate **ransomware attacks, phishing incidents, and insider threats**.

✔ **Implement logging & monitoring tools** – Use **SIEM systems (Splunk, IBM QRadar, Microsoft Sentinel)** to detect **threats**.

✔ **Have a communication plan** – Know **who to notify** (internal teams, regulators, customers).

✔ **Backup critical data regularly** – Use **offline backups** to prevent **ransomware losses**.

📌 **Example:**
A bank **conducts quarterly incident response drills**. After a recent simulation, they identified **gaps in their ransomware containment strategy**. They **updated their backup processes** and improved **incident reporting timelines**.

Lesson: Testing and refining your IR plan is just as important as having one.

Key Takeaways

✔ **Incident Response is crucial for minimizing damage during a cyberattack.**
✔ **The five phases of IR (Preparation, Detection, Containment, Eradication, Post-Incident Review) ensure a structured response.**
✔ **Real-world incidents (Colonial Pipeline, Twitter, Marriott) highlight the need for proactive security measures.**
✔ **Organizations must regularly test and update their IR plans** to stay ahead of threats.

Next Chapter: Cyber Insurance – Managing Risk and Liability

In **Chapter 15,** we'll explore **how businesses can protect themselves financially** against cyberattacks through **cyber insurance policies.**

💰 **A strong defense is critical—but what happens when all else fails? Let's talk cyber insurance!** 🚀

CHAPTER 15

The Role of Security Operations Centers (SOC)

Introduction

As cyber threats grow **more sophisticated and frequent**, businesses need a **centralized team** dedicated to **detecting, responding to, and preventing security incidents**. This is where the **Security Operations Center (SOC)** comes in.

A **SOC is the nerve center** of an organization's cybersecurity efforts, staffed by experts who **monitor networks, investigate threats, and respond to attacks in real-time**.

Why SOCs Matter

✔ **24/7 Security Monitoring** – Cyber threats **never sleep**, so continuous monitoring is essential.
✔ **Faster Incident Response** – SOC teams **detect and contain breaches quickly**, reducing damage.
✔ **Threat Intelligence & Proactive Defense** – SOCs analyze **global cyber threats** to prevent future attacks.

In this chapter, we will explore:

- **What a SOC is and how it operates** – Understanding its structure and functions.
- **SOC analysts vs. security engineers: Who does what?** – The roles within a SOC.
- **Real-world SOC operations** – Case studies from major enterprises.

By the end of this chapter, you'll have a **clear understanding** of how SOCs **protect businesses from cyber threats**.

---

1. What is a Security Operations Center (SOC) and How It Operates?

A **Security Operations Center (SOC)** is a **dedicated cybersecurity team** responsible for **monitoring, detecting, analyzing, and responding to security threats** in real-time.

A. Key Responsibilities of a SOC

◆ **Continuous Network Monitoring** – Tracks **logs, user activity, and system behaviors**.
◆ **Threat Detection & Analysis** – Uses **AI and threat intelligence** to identify risks.
◆ **Incident Response** – Rapidly responds to cyberattacks and contains threats.
◆ **Vulnerability Management** – Finds and fixes security weaknesses.
◆ **Compliance & Reporting** – Ensures adherence to **GDPR, PCI-DSS, ISO 27001** standards.

B. How a SOC Works: The Operational Workflow

The SOC follows a **structured workflow** to handle security incidents efficiently.

Step 1: Threat Detection & Monitoring
☑ Use **SIEM (Security Information & Event Management) tools** like **Splunk, IBM QRadar, and**

141

Microsoft Sentinel to analyze network activity.
☑ Monitor logs from **firewalls, intrusion detection systems (IDS), endpoints, and cloud services**.

Step 2: Incident Triage & Investigation
☑ Analyze alerts to determine if they are **false positives** or real threats.
☑ Identify **attack vectors** (e.g., phishing, malware, insider threats).

Step 3: Containment & Response
☑ Isolate compromised systems to prevent the attack from spreading.
☑ Block malicious IPs, disable compromised accounts, and deploy patches.

Step 4: Remediation & Recovery
☑ Remove malware, close vulnerabilities, and restore affected systems.
☑ Conduct **post-incident analysis** to prevent recurrence.

📌 **Key Takeaway: A well-functioning SOC provides real-time visibility into cyber threats and enables rapid response to attacks.**

---

2. SOC Analysts vs. Security Engineers: Who Does What?

A SOC is staffed by **different cybersecurity professionals**, each with distinct responsibilities.

A. SOC Analysts (Tiers 1, 2, and 3) – The Frontline Defenders

SOC analysts are responsible for **monitoring, detecting, and responding to threats**.

SOC Analyst Tier	Role & Responsibilities	Tools Used
Tier 1: SOC Analyst (Entry-Level)	Monitors security alerts, identifies threats, and escalates issues.	SIEM, IDS/IPS, log analysis tools
Tier 2: Incident Responder	Investigates alerts, contains threats, and performs forensic analysis.	EDR (Endpoint Detection & Response), malware analysis tools
Tier 3: Threat Hunter	Conducts **proactive threat hunting**, finding hidden threats before they strike.	Threat intelligence platforms, advanced analytics

📌 **Example:** A Tier 1 SOC analyst **notices unusual login attempts from Russia**. The **incident responder (Tier 2)** investigates, confirming a **compromised admin account**. The **SOC quickly disables the account** to prevent further damage.

B. Security Engineers – The Builders & Defenders

While SOC analysts **detect and respond** to threats, **security engineers** focus on **building and maintaining** security infrastructure.

✅ Key Responsibilities of Security Engineers:

- Configure **firewalls, SIEM, and endpoint protection tools**.
- Implement **access controls and identity management**.
- Develop **custom detection rules** to spot advanced threats.
- Automate security processes using **SOAR (Security Orchestration, Automation & Response) tools**.

📌 **Key Takeaway: SOC analysts detect and respond to threats, while security engineers build and maintain security systems. Both teams work together to protect the organization.**

---

3. Real-World SOC Operations: Case Studies from Major Enterprises

Case Study 1: Stopping a Ransomware Attack in Progress

Scenario:

A global manufacturing company was targeted by a **ransomware attack**. Attackers had **infected one server**, and the malware was spreading across the network.

SOC Response:

1 Detection:

- SIEM **alerted Tier 1 analysts** about **unusual file encryption** activity.
  2 **Investigation:**
- Tier 2 analysts **identified the ransomware variant** and attack timeline.
  3 **Containment:**
- The SOC **isolated the infected machines** to prevent further damage.
  4 **Eradication & Recovery:**
- Security engineers **deployed a system rollback from backups.**
- The vulnerability **used for initial access was patched.**

☑ **Outcome:** The attack was **neutralized within 90 minutes**, preventing major business disruption.

📌 **Lesson: A fast SOC response prevented a full-scale ransomware disaster.**

Case Study 2: Defending Against a Nation-State Cyber Attack

Scenario:

A **financial institution** detected signs of **sophisticated cyber espionage**.

SOC Response:

1 **Threat Hunting:**

- The Tier 3 team **discovered a hidden backdoor in a server.**
  2 **Forensics & Investigation:**

- Analysts **traced the attack** to a **nation-state-sponsored hacking   group**.
  ③ **Countermeasures:**
- The SOC **removed the backdoor**, strengthened security policies, and blocked **malicious IPs**.

✅ **Outcome:** The attack was **stopped before financial data was stolen**.

📌 **Lesson: Proactive threat hunting can prevent stealthy cyberattacks before they cause harm.**

Case Study 3: A Retail Chain's Struggle with Phishing Attacks

Scenario:

A **large retail chain** faced an increase in **phishing emails** targeting employees.

SOC Response:

① **SIEM flagged multiple login attempts** from suspicious locations.
② **SOC analysts identified compromised accounts** due to **employee   phishing   failures**.
③ **Security engineers implemented:**

- **Stronger email filtering**
- **Mandatory MFA for all employees**
- **Security awareness training**

✅ Outcome: Phishing attack success rates dropped by 75% in six months.

📌 Lesson: SOC teams must focus on both technical security and employee awareness to stop phishing attacks.

---

4. How Businesses Can Improve SOC Operations

To build a **world-class SOC**, businesses must **invest in people, processes, and technology**.

✅ Best Practices for an Effective SOC

✔ **Invest in AI & Automation** – SIEM, SOAR, and AI-driven analytics reduce false positives.
✔ **Train SOC Analysts Continuously** – Keep up with **emerging threats and attack tactics**.
✔ **Use Threat Intelligence** – Monitor **global cyber threats** to anticipate attacks.
✔ **Conduct Regular Red Team vs. Blue Team Exercises** – Improve **attack detection and response**.
✔ **Establish Clear Incident Response Playbooks** – Standardized processes **reduce response time**.

📌 Example: A global e-commerce company **automated 70% of security alerts** using **SOAR tools**, allowing SOC analysts to **focus on high-priority threats**.

Lesson: Automation improves SOC efficiency and reduces analyst burnout.

Key Takeaways

✔ **SOCs are the frontline defenders against cyber threats.**
✔ **SOC analysts detect threats, while security engineers build security infrastructure.**
✔ **Real-world SOC operations show how businesses stop cyberattacks in real-time.**
✔ **AI, automation, and continuous training are essential for an effective SOC.**

Next Chapter: Cyber Insurance – Managing Risk and Liability

In **Chapter 16**, we'll explore how businesses use **cyber insurance** to recover from cyberattacks **financially**.

💰 **Even with strong security, breaches happen—let's talk about financial protection!** 🚀

CHAPTER 16

Threat Intelligence – Predicting and Preventing Attacks

Introduction

Cybercriminals are always evolving, using **new tactics, techniques, and procedures (TTPs)** to bypass security defenses. **Threat Intelligence (TI)** helps organizations **stay ahead of cyber threats** by gathering and analyzing **real-time attack data** to predict and prevent future incidents.

Why Threat Intelligence Matters

✔ **Proactive Defense** – Instead of reacting to attacks, organizations **predict and block them before they occur**.

✔ **Reduces Attack Surface** – Identifies **vulnerable assets and security gaps** before hackers do.

✔ **Improves Incident Response** – Faster detection and mitigation of **real threats**.

In this chapter, we will explore:

- **How organizations gather intelligence on cyber threats** – The sources and methods used.
- **OSINT (Open Source Intelligence) and its role in cybersecurity** – How publicly available data aids in threat analysis.
- **Case study: How threat intelligence stopped a cyber attack before it happened** – A real-world example of proactive defense.

By the end of this chapter, you'll understand how **threat intelligence enables businesses to anticipate and prevent cyberattacks**.

---

1. How Organizations Gather Intelligence on Cyber Threats

A. What is Threat Intelligence?

Threat Intelligence (TI) is the process of collecting, analyzing, and applying **data on cyber threats** to enhance security defenses.

✅ **Types of Threat Intelligence:**

Type	Purpose	Example Use Case
Tactical Intelligence	Focuses on **immediate threats** (IPs, malware signatures).	Blocking known **malicious IPs and domains**.
Operational Intelligence	Provides details on **ongoing attacks** (attack methods, TTPs).	Detecting active **phishing campaigns** targeting employees.
Strategic Intelligence	High-level analysis of **threat trends and geopolitical risks**.	Identifying **nation-state-sponsored cyberattacks**.

📌 **Key Takeaway: Threat Intelligence transforms raw data into actionable security measures.**

150

B. Sources of Threat Intelligence

Threat intelligence comes from multiple sources, including **public, private, and government data feeds**.

Source	Description	Examples
OSINT (Open Source Intelligence)	Publicly available data on threats.	Twitter, blogs, WHOIS records.
Dark Web Monitoring	Tracking hacker forums and underground markets.	Stolen credentials, ransomware leaks.
Threat Intelligence Feeds	Realtime feeds with **malicious IPs, domains, and file hashes**.	IBM X-Force, FireEye, Cisco Talos.
Security Vendors & Researchers	Reports from cybersecurity companies.	Kaspersky, CrowdStrike, Palo Alto Networks.
Government & Law Enforcement	Cyber threat advisories from agencies.	FBI, NSA, Europol.

📌 **Example:**
After the **SolarWinds cyber attack, threat intelligence feeds** helped companies **identify and block the attackers' domains**.

C. How Threat Intelligence Improves Cybersecurity

☑ **Prevents Cyber Attacks** – Blocks **malicious IPs, emails, and domains** before they cause damage.
☑ **Enhances SOC Operations** – Helps SOC analysts **quickly detect and respond** to active threats.
☑ **Strengthens Vulnerability Management** – Prioritizes **patching based on real-world threats**.

📌 **Example:**
A **financial institution integrated threat intelligence feeds** into their **SIEM system**. When attackers **tried to access systems from a blacklisted IP**, the SOC **automatically blocked the request**.

Lesson: Real-time threat intelligence enables automated, proactive defense.

2. OSINT (Open Source Intelligence) and Its Role in Cybersecurity

Open Source Intelligence (OSINT) is the collection of publicly available information to identify cyber threats. Hackers also use OSINT for **reconnaissance** before launching attacks.

A. How OSINT is Used in Cybersecurity

☑ **Attackers use OSINT for Reconnaissance**

- Hackers gather **employee email addresses** from **LinkedIn** for phishing attacks.
- Domain lookups via **WHOIS records** reveal **company infrastructure details**.

☑ **Defenders use OSINT to Identify Threats**

- SOC analysts **track dark web activity** for **stolen credentials**.
- OSINT tools scan **exposed corporate data** on GitHub and public forums.

B. Popular OSINT Tools for Threat Intelligence

Tool	Function
Shodan	Finds **internet-exposed devices and vulnerabilities**.
theHarvester	Collects **emails, subdomains, and IPs** from public sources.
Maltego	Maps relationships between **threat actors, companies, and domains**.
SpiderFoot	Automates OSINT scanning across **multiple data sources**.

📌 **Example:**
A **cybersecurity firm used Shodan** to discover that a **major retailer had thousands of exposed servers** online, reducing their attack surface before hackers exploited them.

153

Lesson: Hackers use OSINT for attacks—organizations must use OSINT to defend themselves.

---

3. Case Study: How Threat Intelligence Stopped a Cyber Attack Before It Happened

Case Study: Preventing a Ransomware Attack

Scenario:

A global healthcare provider was targeted by **ransomware operators**. However, **threat intelligence analysts detected early warning signs** before the attack occurred.

Threat Intelligence Discovery:

① **Dark Web Monitoring:** Analysts found **hackers discussing vulnerabilities** in the company's infrastructure.
② **OSINT Analysis:** The attackers **scanned the company's IP addresses** looking for weaknesses.
③ **Threat Intelligence Feeds:** Identified **known ransomware domains** communicating with the company's network.

Proactive Defense Actions:

☑ **Blocked malicious IPs** before attackers could exploit vulnerabilities.
☑ **Updated firewall rules** to prevent unauthorized access.
☑ **Patched vulnerable systems** before ransomware could be deployed.

154

☑ **Trained employees on phishing awareness**, reducing the chance of social engineering attacks.

Outcome:

The **ransomware attack was stopped before it could be launched**.

📌 **Lesson: Threat intelligence enables proactive defense, stopping attacks before they cause harm.**

---

4. How Businesses Can Leverage Threat Intelligence

☑ **Steps to Implement an Effective Threat Intelligence Program**

✔ **Integrate threat intelligence feeds** into **firewalls, SIEM, and endpoint security**.
✔ **Monitor dark web activity** for **leaked employee credentials**.
✔ **Use OSINT tools** to scan for **exposed company data**.
✔ **Collaborate with global cybersecurity communities** for intelligence sharing.
✔ **Train employees on emerging cyber threats** (e.g., AI-driven phishing scams).

📌 **Example:**
A multinational corporation **automated threat intelligence processing**, reducing **false positives by 60%** and improving **threat detection response times**.

155

Lesson: Automating threat intelligence improves efficiency and security.

Key Takeaways

✔ **Threat intelligence helps predict and prevent cyber attacks.**
✔ **OSINT plays a critical role in identifying threats before hackers strike.**
✔ **Dark web monitoring and real-time intelligence feeds enhance cybersecurity defenses.**
✔ **A healthcare company stopped a ransomware attack by leveraging threat intelligence.**
✔ **Automating threat intelligence improves security efficiency.**

Next Chapter: Cybersecurity in Artificial Intelligence – Securing AI Systems

In **Chapter 17**, we'll explore **how AI is revolutionizing cybersecurity—and why attackers are also using AI for cybercrime**.

🤖 **AI is shaping the future of cybersecurity—let's dive in!** 🚀

CHAPTER 17

Zero Trust Security – Eliminating Implicit Trust

Introduction

Traditional cybersecurity models rely on **perimeter-based defenses**, where users and devices inside a network are **implicitly trusted**. However, this approach **no longer works** in modern environments, where attackers often gain access through **phishing, credential theft, or insider threats**.

Zero Trust Security (ZTS) eliminates **implicit trust** and requires **continuous verification** of users, devices, and network activities. **No one is trusted by default—not even employees inside the network.**

Why Zero Trust Matters

✔ **Stops Insider Threats** – No automatic access, even for employees.
✔ **Prevents Lateral Movement** – Attackers can't move freely inside the network.
✔ **Strengthens Identity Security** – Requires **continuous authentication** and device verification.

In this chapter, we'll cover:

- **What Zero Trust is and how it works** – The core principles of this security model.

- **Implementing Zero Trust in a corporate environment** – Step-by-step integration.
- **The future of Zero Trust and network security** – How ZTS will shape cybersecurity.

By the end of this chapter, you'll understand **why Zero Trust is replacing traditional security models** and how businesses can **implement it effectively**.

1. What is Zero Trust, and How Does It Work?

A. Understanding the Zero Trust Model

Zero Trust is a security framework that assumes "trust no one"—every request must be verified before access is granted.

Unlike traditional security models, which rely on **firewalls and VPNs** to protect internal networks, Zero Trust focuses on **identity verification, device security, and least privilege access**.

✅ **Key Principles of Zero Trust:**

Principle	Description
Never Trust, Always Verify	Every request (user or device) must be authenticated and authorized before access is granted.
Least Privilege Access	Users and devices get only **the minimum access needed** to do their job.

Principle	Description
Microsegmentation	Network access is divided into **smaller zones** to prevent attackers from moving freely.
Continuous Monitoring	Logs, analytics, and AI are used to **detect suspicious activity in real time**.
Multi-Factor Authentication (MFA)	Every login attempt requires additional authentication factors beyond a password.

📌 **Example:**
A **Zero Trust-enabled network** requires **every device and user** to be authenticated **every time they attempt to access a resource**, even if they are already inside the network.

B. How Zero Trust Differs from Traditional Security

Traditional Security	Zero Trust Security
"Trust but verify"	**"Never trust, always verify"**
Relies on **firewalls & VPNs**	Uses **identity-based access controls**
Full network access once inside	Access is **restricted and monitored**

Traditional Security	Zero Trust Security
Flat network (attackers can move laterally)	Uses **microsegmentation** to prevent lateral movement

📌 **Key Takeaway: Zero Trust prevents attackers from gaining unrestricted access—even if they bypass the perimeter.**

---

2. Implementing Zero Trust in a Corporate Environment

Transitioning to **Zero Trust Security** requires **strategic planning** and a **step-by-step implementation process**.

A. Step 1: Identify & Classify Critical Assets

1. Identify **sensitive data, applications, and systems** that require strict access control.
2. Categorize assets by **risk level** (e.g., HR databases, customer records, financial data).

B. Step 2: Verify Identities with Multi-Factor Authentication (MFA)

1. Require MFA for all users, including employees and third-party vendors.
2. Implement **passwordless authentication** (e.g., biometrics, hardware tokens).

📌 **Example:**
A financial institution **implemented MFA** for all remote workers. **Phishing attacks dropped by 85%**, preventing unauthorized access.

C. Step 3: Enforce Least Privilege Access

1. Define **who needs access to what** based on job roles.
2. Use **Role-Based Access Control (RBAC)** and **Just-In-Time (JIT) Access** (temporary permissions).
3. Remove **excessive admin privileges** to reduce insider threat risks.

📌 **Example:**
A tech company **restricted admin access** to sensitive data. If employees needed temporary access, they **requested approval via a secure portal**.

D. Step 4: Implement Microsegmentation

1. Divide the network into **isolated security zones** (e.g., finance, HR, IT).
2. Restrict access **between segments**—even for employees.
3. Use **Software-Defined Perimeters (SDP)** to create **invisible network boundaries**.

📌 **Example:**
A healthcare provider **segmented patient records** from general hospital networks. Even if an attacker breached **one system, they couldn't access medical records**.

E. Step 5: Use AI & Analytics for Continuous Monitoring

1 Deploy **SIEM (Security Information & Event Management)** to **analyze security logs in real-time**.
2 Implement **User Behavior Analytics (UBA)** to detect suspicious   activities.
3 Automate **threat response** with **SOAR (Security Orchestration, Automation, and Response)**.

📌   **Example:**
An e-commerce company used **AI-driven anomaly detection**. When a hacker **logged in from an unusual location**, the system **automatically blocked access** and alerted security teams.

3. The Future of Zero Trust and Network Security

A. How Zero Trust Will Evolve

✅ **AI & Automation** – AI will detect suspicious activity **instantly**   and   block   access.
✅ **Passwordless Authentication** – Businesses will move to   **biometrics   and   hardware   tokens**.
✅ **Cloud-Native Zero Trust** – Security will be built into **cloud   environments   from   the   start**.
✅ **5G & IoT Security** – Zero Trust will protect **connected devices and smart networks**.

📌 **Example:**
Google's **BeyondCorp Zero Trust model** eliminated VPNs. Employees now authenticate via **device trust and AI-driven risk scoring**.

B. Why Zero Trust is Critical for Cybersecurity

1 **Remote Work & Cloud Adoption** – Employees access data **from anywhere**, increasing attack risks.
2 **Ransomware & Insider Threats** – Attackers **bypass traditional defenses** using **stolen credentials**.
3 **Regulatory Compliance** – GDPR, NIST, and ISO 27001 **recommend Zero Trust principles**.

📌 **Example:**
A global retail company adopted **Zero Trust for supply chain security**. Even if a **supplier's system was hacked, attackers couldn't access the company's data**.

---

4. Steps to Start Implementing Zero Trust Today

✔ Action Plan for Businesses

✔ **Require Multi-Factor Authentication (MFA)** for all employees.
✔ **Implement Least Privilege Access** (reduce admin accounts).
✔ **Segment networks to prevent lateral movement.**
✔ **Monitor user behavior & automate threat detection.**

✔ **Replace VPNs with Zero Trust Network Access (ZTNA)** solutions.

📌 **Example:**
A large enterprise **phased out VPNs and moved to ZTNA**. As a result, **zero trust access controls reduced phishing-related breaches by 90%**.

Key Takeaways

✔ **Zero Trust eliminates implicit trust and requires continuous   verification.**
✔ **Unlike traditional security, Zero Trust focuses on identity, least privilege, and microsegmentation.**
✔ **Implementing MFA, network segmentation, and AI-driven monitoring is key to Zero Trust.**
✔ **Zero Trust is the future of cybersecurity, especially for remote work and cloud environments.**

Next Chapter: Cybersecurity in Artificial Intelligence – Securing AI Systems

In **Chapter 18**, we'll explore how **AI is transforming cybersecurity**—and why hackers are also using AI for **automated cybercrime**.

👹 **Can AI defend against AI-powered attacks? Let's find out!**

CHAPTER 18

AI and Machine Learning in Cybersecurity

Introduction

As cyber threats become **more sophisticated and automated**, traditional security methods struggle to keep up. **Artificial Intelligence (AI) and Machine Learning (ML)** have become **essential tools** in modern cybersecurity, helping organizations detect and respond to threats **faster and more accurately**.

At the same time, **cybercriminals are also using AI** to launch **automated, intelligent attacks**, making cybersecurity a constant **arms race** between defenders and attackers.

Why AI Matters in Cybersecurity

✔ **Detects threats in real-time** – AI analyzes **billions of security events per second**.
✔ **Predicts & prevents attacks** – AI-powered systems recognize **patterns of cybercrime** before they escalate.
✔ **Automates security responses** – AI can **block, quarantine, or neutralize** threats without human intervention.

In this chapter, we'll explore:

- **How AI is being used in cybersecurity (and by hackers!)** – The double-edged sword of AI.

- **AI-driven malware detection and anomaly detection** – How AI identifies hidden threats.
- **Real-world examples: AI security tools in action** – How AI is defending businesses today.

By the end of this chapter, you'll understand how **AI is transforming cybersecurity** and how organizations can **leverage AI while defending against AI-powered attacks**.

1. How AI is Being Used in Cybersecurity (and by Hackers!)

A. How Defenders Use AI in Cybersecurity

AI enhances **cyber defense strategies** by automating threat detection and response.

✅ Key AI Applications in Cybersecurity:

AI Use Case	How It Works	Example
Threat Detection & Prevention	AI scans network traffic and identifies anomalies in real-time.	Detecting a **DDoS attack before it impacts services**.
Phishing & Email Security	AI detects phishing emails by analyzing language patterns and sender behavior.	**Microsoft Defender blocks phishing emails before employees see them**.

AI Use Case	How It Works	Example
Behavioral Analytics	AI monitors user behavior to detect insider threats or compromised accounts.	Detecting suspicious login attempts from unusual locations.
Incident Response Automation	AI-driven security tools contain attacks automatically.	AI-powered SOAR tools isolate an infected endpoint before malware spreads.
Vulnerability Management	AI predicts which software vulnerabilities are most likely to be exploited.	AI prioritizes patching the most critical security flaws first.

 Example:
A **global bank** used AI-driven analytics to **detect unusual transactions** in real-time, preventing **$10 million in fraud** within the first year of implementation.

B. How Hackers Are Using AI for Cybercrime

Cybercriminals **also leverage AI** to automate and enhance their attacks.

☑ **How Hackers Use AI:**

AI-Powered Attack	How It Works	Example
AI-Generated Phishing Emails	AI crafts **convincing phishing emails** by mimicking writing styles.	Hackers use AI to **impersonate a CEO in business email compromise (BEC) scams**.
Deepfake Cyber Attacks	AI-generated **fake audio/video** manipulates people into **revealing sensitive data**.	A deepfake **CEO voice** tricked employees into wiring **$243,000 to attackers**.
AI-Powered Malware	AI-based malware **adapts and evolves to** bypass antivirus programs.	**"DeepLocker" malware** stays undetected until triggered by a **specific target**.
AI-Enhanced Password Cracking	AI speeds up brute-force attacks, cracking passwords in **seconds**.	Hackers use AI to **instantly break weak passwords** with massive computing power.
Automated Bot Attacks	AI-driven bots **scan for vulnerabilities** and launch attacks automatically.	AI bots **find and exploit unpatched web servers** without human intervention.

📌 **Example:**
In **2021, a deepfake phishing scam used AI-generated**

voice technology to impersonate a company executive, convincing an employee to transfer $35 million.

Lesson: AI is a powerful cybersecurity tool—but in the wrong hands, it becomes a dangerous weapon.

---

2. AI-Driven Malware Detection and Anomaly Detection

AI is particularly effective at detecting advanced cyber threats that evade traditional security tools.

A. AI-Powered Malware Detection

Traditional antivirus software relies on signature-based detection, meaning it only stops known threats. AI, however, can detect new and unknown malware by analyzing behavioral patterns.

✅ How AI Detects Malware: ① Analyzes file behavior instead of relying on known signatures.
② Uses machine learning algorithms to identify malware variants.
③ Detects zero-day attacks by recognizing suspicious activity.

📌   Example: Cylance, an AI-driven antivirus company, detected new malware strains 99% faster than traditional antivirus programs.

Lesson: AI improves cybersecurity by detecting never-before-seen threats.

B. AI-Powered Anomaly Detection

AI excels at **finding unusual activity** in vast amounts of security data.

☑ **How AI Detects Anomalies:** ✔ **User Behavior Analytics (UBA)** – AI learns **normal user behavior** and flags unusual actions. ✔ **Network Traffic Analysis (NTA)** – AI detects **strange data patterns, like sudden data transfers**. ✔ **Endpoint Detection & Response (EDR)** – AI **identifies compromised devices** before major damage occurs.

📌 **Example:** A **healthcare provider** used AI-powered behavioral analytics to **detect an insider stealing patient records**, preventing a **major data breach**.

Lesson: AI helps detect insider threats and suspicious activities before they escalate.

3. Real-World Examples: AI Security Tools in Action

A. AI-Powered Cybersecurity Tools

Organizations **worldwide** are adopting **AI security solutions** to combat evolving threats.

☑ **Top AI Cybersecurity Tools & Their Use Cases:**

AI Security Tool	Function	Used By
Darktrace	Uses AI for **network anomaly detection**.	Financial institutions, governments.
Microsoft Defender AI	AI-driven **threat detection & response**.	Enterprises worldwide.
IBM Watson for Cybersecurity	AI-powered **threat intelligence platform**.	Fortune 500 companies.
CrowdStrike Falcon	AI-based **endpoint detection & response (EDR)**.	Cloud providers, tech companies.
Google Chronicle	AI-enhanced **SIEM platform for log analysis**.	Large enterprises.

📌 **Example:** A **Fortune 500 company implemented AI-based endpoint protection (CrowdStrike Falcon)** and **prevented a zero-day ransomware attack** before it spread.

Lesson: AI-powered cybersecurity tools provide an essential defense against modern cyber threats.

---

4. The Future of AI in Cybersecurity

As AI continues to evolve, **its role in cybersecurity will expand** in both **defensive and offensive capabilities**.

✅ Predictions for the Future of AI Security

✔ **Self-Healing Security Systems** – AI will **automatically patch vulnerabilities** before they are exploited.
✔ **AI-Powered SOCs (Security Operations Centers)** – AI will **automate 90% of security alerts**, reducing analyst burnout.
✔ **Adversarial AI Warfare** – AI-driven cyberattacks will become **more advanced, requiring AI-powered defenses**.
✔ **AI for Threat Hunting** – AI will actively **search for hidden cyber threats** in real time.

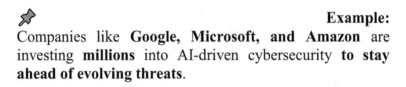 **Example:** Companies like **Google, Microsoft, and Amazon** are investing **millions** into AI-driven cybersecurity **to stay ahead of evolving threats**.

Key Takeaways

✔ **AI is revolutionizing cybersecurity by detecting and preventing attacks in real-time.**
✔ **Hackers are also using AI for automated, adaptive cybercrime.**
✔ **AI-powered tools improve malware detection, anomaly detection, and incident response.**
✔ **Companies using AI-driven cybersecurity tools can block threats before they cause damage.**
✔ **The future of cybersecurity will be a battle of AI vs. AI.**

Next Chapter: The Rise of Quantum Computing and Its Impact on Cybersecurity

In **Chapter 19**, we'll explore how **quantum computing is reshaping encryption, cybersecurity, and cryptographic security**.

⚛ **Is quantum computing the next big cybersecurity breakthrough—or the biggest threat? Let's find out!**

CHAPTER 19

Protecting Your Online Identity

Introduction

In the digital world, **your personal information is a valuable target for hackers**. From **data breaches** to **identity theft**, cybercriminals use stolen data to commit fraud, access bank accounts, and even impersonate individuals.

If your identity is stolen, it can take years to recover. Protecting your online identity is no longer optional—it's **a necessity**.

Why Online Identity Protection Matters

✔ **Identity theft costs billions** – In 2022 alone, identity theft resulted in **$52 billion in losses** worldwide.
✔ **Hackers exploit personal data** – A **single stolen password** can lead to **multiple account breaches**.
✔ **Data breaches expose private information** – Even if you're careful, **companies storing your data can get hacked**.

In this chapter, we will explore:

- **The dangers of data breaches and identity theft** – How cybercriminals steal and misuse personal data.
- **Best practices for securing personal accounts** – Actionable steps to protect yourself.
- **Case study: How a hacker stole someone's identity in 5 minutes** – A real-world example of identity theft.

By the end of this chapter, you'll know **how to protect your personal information** and **prevent hackers from stealing your identity**.

1. The Dangers of Data Breaches and Identity Theft

A. How Hackers Steal Personal Data

Cybercriminals **use various techniques** to steal personal information and commit fraud.

Attack Type	How It Works	Example
Phishing Attacks	Hackers send fake emails pretending to be **banks, social media platforms, or employers** to steal login credentials.	A fake PayPal email tricks users into entering their passwords.
Data Breaches	Hackers break into company databases and steal personal information, including **names, emails, passwords, and credit card numbers**.	The Equifax breach (2017) exposed **147 million people's data**.
Credential Stuffing	Hackers use stolen passwords from one site to log into other accounts, taking advantage of password reuse.	A hacker uses a leaked Netflix password to access the victim's bank account.

Attack Type	How It Works	Example
SIM Swapping	Attackers convince a mobile carrier to transfer a victim's phone number to their SIM card, gaining access to SMS-based two-factor authentication (2FA).	A hacker **steals cryptocurrency** by intercepting 2FA codes sent via SMS.
Dark Web Sales	Stolen personal data is sold on hacker forums and the **dark web** for as little as $1 per account.	A hacker buys **social security numbers and bank details** to commit fraud.

📌 **Example:** In 2021, hackers leaked **533 million Facebook user records** online, including phone numbers and email addresses. **Cybercriminals used this data for phishing attacks and identity fraud.**

Lesson: Even if you're cautious, your data can be stolen in a company breach. Proactive security is essential.

---

2. Best Practices for Securing Personal Accounts

To protect yourself from **identity theft and online fraud**, follow these best practices.

A. Use Strong, Unique Passwords for Every Account

◆ **Do NOT reuse passwords** across multiple sites.

◆ Use a **password manager** (e.g., Bitwarden, 1Password, LastPass) to generate and store **unique, complex passwords**.

◆ Ensure passwords are at least **14+ characters long**, mixing uppercase, lowercase, numbers, and symbols.

📌 **Example:**
Instead of using **"Password123"**, use a password manager to generate **"gT!8vL@9r$0Pz!mD"**.

Lesson: A strong, unique password prevents credential stuffing attacks.

B. Enable Multi-Factor Authentication (MFA)

Multi-Factor Authentication (MFA) adds an extra security layer by requiring **a second factor** (e.g., an app-generated code or biometric verification) in addition to a password.

☑ **Best MFA Practices:** ✔ Use **app-based authentication (e.g., Google Authenticator, Authy)** instead of SMS (which is vulnerable to SIM swapping).

✔ Enable MFA on **all important accounts**, including email, banking, and social media.

📌 **Example:**
A hacker obtains your Netflix password from a data breach but **cannot log in** because you enabled MFA.

Lesson: Even if your password is stolen, MFA prevents unauthorized access.

C. Secure Your Email Account – It's the Gateway to Everything

Your **email account is the key to all other accounts**. If hackers access it, they can **reset passwords** and **take over other services**.

✅ **How to Secure Your Email:** ✔ **Use a strong password and MFA** (email is a top hacking target). ✔ **Review email forwarding rules** to ensure no one secretly receives your messages. ✔ **Avoid clicking unknown links** in emails—even if they look legitimate.

📌 **Example:** A hacker **gains access to an email account** and uses **password resets** to take over bank, shopping, and social media accounts.

Lesson: Your email security affects ALL your accounts—secure it well!

D. Check if Your Data Has Been Breached

Use **Have I Been Pwned** (https://haveibeenpwned.com/) to check if your **email or phone number** has been leaked in a data breach.

✅ **What to Do If Your Data Was Breached:** ✔ **Change your password immediately** (and use a unique one).

✔ **Enable MFA** to prevent unauthorized logins.
✔ **Monitor your accounts** for suspicious activity.

📌 **Example:**
A user finds their **email and password** in a leaked database from a **LinkedIn data breach**. **By changing their password immediately, they prevent hackers from accessing their account.**

Lesson: Regularly check if your data has been leaked and take action!

E. Protect Your Personal Information on Social Media

Hackers **use social media** to gather personal details for phishing, impersonation, or social engineering attacks.

☑ **Social Media Security Tips: ✔ Set profiles to private** and limit public information.
✔ **Do not post birthdates, addresses, or phone numbers** online.
✔ **Avoid answering "fun quizzes"** that ask for personal details (e.g., "Your first pet's name" = security question answer).

📌 **Example:**
A hacker **finds a user's birthday and high school name** on Facebook, then **guesses their bank security question** to reset their account password.

Lesson: Sharing personal details online can help hackers steal your identity.

---

3. Case Study: How a Hacker Stole Someone's Identity in 5 Minutes

The Attack

◆ A hacker **finds an old password from a LinkedIn breach** on the dark web.
◆ They **use credential stuffing** to log into the victim's email account (same password used).
◆ The hacker **resets banking and social media passwords** using email access.
◆ Within **5 minutes**, the hacker **steals $2,000**, posts scams on the victim's Facebook, and **locks them out of all accounts**.

How This Could Have Been Prevented

✅ **Use unique passwords for each account** (prevents credential stuffing).
✅ **Enable MFA on email** (blocks unauthorized access).
✅ **Monitor for data breaches** and change compromised passwords immediately.

📌 Key Takeaway:
💡 **One weak password can lead to complete identity theft.**

---

4. Summary: How to Protect Your Online Identity

✅ Checklist for Identity Protection

✔ **Use a password manager** to generate strong, unique passwords.

✔ **Enable MFA on all critical accounts** (email, banking, social media).

✔ **Check if your data has been leaked** via HaveIBeenPwned.

✔ **Secure your email account** (the gateway to all other accounts).

✔ **Be cautious on social media**—avoid sharing sensitive personal details.

✔ **Monitor bank and credit card statements** for unauthorized activity.

✔ **Use identity theft protection services** (optional, but useful).

📌 **Final Thought:** **Your personal data is valuable—hackers want it. Stay proactive, secure your accounts, and protect your online identity.**

Next Chapter: Securing Your Smart Devices – Protecting IoT from Cyber Attacks

In **Chapter 20**, we'll explore how to **secure smart home devices, IoT security risks, and best practices to prevent cyber intrusions**.

🏠 **Is your smart home secure? Let's find out!**

CHAPTER 20

Social Media Security – Avoiding Digital Exploitation

Introduction

Social media connects billions of people worldwide, but it also exposes users to **cybercriminals, scammers, and digital exploitation**. Attackers use social platforms to **steal personal information, spread malware, and manipulate victims into scams**.

With just a few clicks, **your personal data, photos, and conversations can be misused**—leading to **identity theft, financial fraud, or reputational damage**.

Why Social Media Security Matters

✔ **Your data is valuable** – Hackers **scrape personal details** to exploit users for fraud.
✔ **Social engineering is easier than ever** – Attackers use **public information** to craft convincing scams.
✔ **Once data is exposed, it's permanent** – Deleting posts doesn't erase **screenshots or cached copies**.

In this chapter, we'll explore:

- **How attackers exploit social media for cybercrime** – Common threats and tactics.
- **Privacy settings and personal data protection** – Steps to safeguard your accounts.
- **Real-world example: How a social media scam cost thousands** – A case study of digital deception.

By the end of this chapter, you'll understand how to **protect your social media accounts, avoid scams, and control your online presence**.

---

1. How Attackers Exploit Social Media for Cybercrime

Cybercriminals **leverage social media** to **steal identities, trick victims into scams, and even breach company networks**.

A. Common Social Media Cyber Threats

Threat Type	How It Works	Example
Phishing Scams	Attackers impersonate legitimate brands or friends, tricking users into clicking malicious links.	A fake Instagram message says, "You've won a prize! Click here to claim."
Fake Profiles & Impersonation	Criminals create fake accounts, impersonate people, or take over hacked accounts.	A hacker **pretends to be your friend**, asks for money, or spreads scams.
Malware in Links & Attachments	Clicking a malicious link infects your device with spyware or ransomware.	A Twitter DM claims, "Check out this video of you!"— but leads to malware.
Data Scraping & Identity Theft	Hackers collect **publicly available information** to steal	A scammer finds your birthdate and

Threat Type	How It Works	Example
	identities or answer security questions.	uses it to **reset your bank password**.
Romance & Financial Scams	Criminals manipulate victims into sending money by pretending to be in distress.	A scammer on Facebook pretends to be **a soldier needing urgent funds**.
Deepfake & AI-Manipulated Videos	AI-generated videos make it seem like someone is saying or doing something they never did.	A deepfake impersonates a CEO, convincing employees to transfer money.

📌 **Example:**
In 2023, an AI-generated **deepfake video of Elon Musk** promoted a cryptocurrency scam. Thousands of people **sent money**, believing it was an official endorsement.

Lesson: Social media fraud is evolving—users must stay vigilant.

---

2. Privacy Settings and Personal Data Protection

A. Lock Down Your Social Media Accounts

Attackers use **publicly available information** for scams. **Review and adjust privacy settings** to limit who can see your data.

✅ **Essential Privacy Settings for Every Social Media Account:** ⬜Set **profiles to private** – Only allow trusted connections to see your posts.
②**Limit who can send you friend/follow requests** – Prevent fake accounts from adding you.
③**Disable location sharing** – Avoid exposing your real-time whereabouts.
④**Restrict who can tag you in photos or posts** – Prevent unauthorized content on your timeline.
⑤**Turn off face recognition** – Stop social platforms from auto-tagging your photos.

📌   **Example:**
A woman shared vacation photos **while still abroad**. Thieves saw her location and **robbed her home**, knowing she was away.

Lesson: Never share travel plans in real-time—post photos after you return.

B. Protect Your Personal Data on Social Media

Even if your account is private, **third-party apps, data brokers, and breaches can expose your information.**

✅ **Best Practices for Data Protection:** ✔ **Avoid sharing sensitive details** (birthdate, address, phone number).
✔ **Don't overshare** about your job, family, or daily routine (hackers use this info).
✔ **Delete old accounts** you no longer use (they may still contain personal data).
✔ **Review app permissions** – Revoke access for apps that

don't need your social media data.

✔ **Be cautious with quizzes & viral trends** – Questions like "What's your first pet's name?" can be used to guess security answers.

📌 **Example:**
A viral Facebook game asked users to **post their "superhero name"** using **their first pet's name and mother's maiden name**. These are **common security questions** used to reset accounts.

Lesson: Fun quizzes can be social engineering traps— think before you share!

C. Use Strong Security Measures

✅ **How to Secure Your Social Media Accounts:** ✔ **Use unique, strong passwords** for each platform (consider a password manager).

✔ **Enable Multi-Factor Authentication (MFA)** to prevent unauthorized logins.

✔ **Beware of suspicious friend requests**—verify identities before accepting.

✔ **Never click suspicious links in messages**—hover over URLs before opening.

✔ **Log out of social media on public or shared devices.**

📌 **Example:**
A hacker **guessed a weak Facebook password**, then **reset the victim's email and PayPal accounts**—stealing $5,000.

Lesson: A compromised social media account can lead to full-scale identity theft.

---

3. Real-World Example: How a Social Media Scam Cost Thousands

Case Study: A Facebook Marketplace Scam

The Scam

1. A seller listed **a laptop on Facebook Marketplace** for $800.
2. A buyer contacted them, offering to **pay via a mobile payment app (Zelle, Venmo, or PayPal Friends & Family)**.
3. The buyer sent a **fake email receipt**, claiming payment was   processed.
4. The seller shipped the laptop **before verifying payment**.
5. The money never arrived—**the scammer disappeared with the laptop**.

How the Victim Lost Money

- **They trusted a "buyer" without verifying payment.**
- **They accepted an unprotected payment method (PayPal Friends & Family, which lacks buyer protection).**
- **The scammer used a fake email to make the transaction look legitimate.**

✅   **How   to   Avoid   This   Scam:**
✔ **Only accept verified payments** (avoid wire transfers or unprotected   transactions).

✔ **Verify payment in your account before shipping an item.**

✔ **Meet in a safe, public location** (like a police station for in-person sales).

✔ **Use platforms that offer buyer/seller protection.**

📌 **Lesson: Scammers prey on urgency and trust— always verify before sending money or products.**

---

4. Summary: How to Stay Safe on Social Media

✅ Checklist for Social Media Security

✔ **Set profiles to private** and control what information is public.

✔ **Use strong passwords and enable MFA** on all accounts.

✔ **Never click suspicious links in DMs, emails, or comments.**

✔ **Beware of impersonation scams**—verify identities before sending money.

✔ **Think before you post**—avoid sharing sensitive information.

✔ **Monitor login activity** and remove access to suspicious third-party apps.

✔ **Be skeptical of giveaways, job offers, or investment opportunities.**

📌 **Final Thought: Social media is a powerful tool—but without proper security, it can be a hacker's playground. Protect your digital identity before it's too late.**

Next Chapter: Securing Your Smart Devices – Protecting IoT from Cyber Attacks

In **Chapter 21**, we'll explore **how to protect smart home devices, IoT security risks, and best practices to prevent cyber intrusions**.

⌂ **Is your smart home vulnerable to hackers? Let's find out!**

CHAPTER 21

Cybersecurity for Remote Work and Digital Nomads

Introduction

Remote work has **transformed the modern workforce**, offering flexibility and freedom. However, it also introduces **serious cybersecurity risks. Without corporate firewalls, secure office networks, and IT oversight, remote workers and digital nomads are prime targets for cybercriminals.**

Attackers exploit **weak passwords, unsecured public Wi-Fi, and personal devices** to gain access to sensitive company data, financial accounts, and private communications.

Why Remote Work Security Matters

✔ **Cyberattacks on remote workers increased by 238%** after the shift to hybrid work.
✔ **91% of companies have experienced a remote work security breach.**
✔ **Remote employees are 3x more likely to be targeted by phishing and malware attacks.**

In this chapter, we'll explore:

- **The security risks of working remotely** – How hackers exploit remote environments.
- **VPNs, secure connections, and personal device management** – Best practices for staying safe online.

- **Real-world attack: A compromised remote worker's device** – How poor security led to a company-wide breach.

By the end of this chapter, you'll understand **how to protect yourself while working remotely, whether from home, a café, or across the world as a digital nomad.**

1. The Security Risks of Working Remotely

Remote workers and digital nomads face unique cybersecurity threats because they often use **personal devices, public networks, and cloud-based services**.

A. Common Cyber Threats for Remote Workers

Threat	How It Works	Example
Unsecured Public Wi-Fi	Hackers set up fake "Free Wi-Fi" hotspots to steal login credentials.	A remote worker logs into "CoffeeShop_WiFi," unknowingly connecting to a hacker's device.
Phishing Attacks	Fake emails trick employees into revealing credentials.	A digital nomad receives a fake **"Dropbox login request"** and enters their company password.
Malware & Ransomware	Malicious files infect personal devices, locking or stealing data.	A remote worker downloads a **PDF invoice attachment** that installs ransomware.

192

Threat	How It Works	Example
Weak or Reused Passwords	Attackers brute-force or guess passwords to access corporate accounts.	A hacker logs into a cloud app because the employee reused their **old Facebook password**.
Unpatched Software	Outdated apps contain security flaws that hackers exploit.	A remote worker's **unpatched Zoom client** allows hackers to eavesdrop on meetings.
Lost or Stolen Devices	Laptops and phones without encryption are easy targets.	A traveler leaves their laptop in a **hotel lobby**—attackers access unprotected files.

📌 **Example:** A **financial analyst working from home** received an email from "HR" asking them to verify their payroll details. The email contained a fake link that **stole their credentials**, allowing attackers to access **company banking information**.

Lesson: Remote work requires extra caution—phishing, weak passwords, and unsecured networks are top threats.

2. VPNs, Secure Connections, and Personal Device Management

To protect against cyber threats, remote workers need **secure internet connections, strong authentication, and device management protocols**.

A. Using a VPN for Secure Internet Access

A **Virtual Private Network (VPN)** encrypts your internet traffic, **hiding your location and protecting data** from hackers on public Wi-Fi.

✔ **VPN Best Practices:**
✔ Use a **trusted VPN provider** (NordVPN, ExpressVPN, ProtonVPN).
✔ Avoid **free VPNs** (many log and sell user data).
✔ Always enable **auto-connect** on startup to prevent accidental exposure.

📌 **Example:**
A digital marketer worked from a **co-working space in Thailand** without a VPN. Hackers intercepted their traffic and stole **customer login credentials**.

Lesson: Always use a VPN when working remotely— especially on public Wi-Fi.

B. Managing Personal Devices for Security

Most remote workers use **personal laptops, tablets, and smartphones**, which may lack enterprise-grade security.

☑ **How to Secure Personal Devices:**
✔ **Use full-disk encryption** (BitLocker for Windows, FileVault for Mac).
✔ **Keep software & OS updated**—patch vulnerabilities immediately.
✔ **Install endpoint protection (antivirus, firewall, and anti-malware software).**
✔ **Enable remote wipe** in case a device is lost or stolen.

📌 **Example:**
A journalist's **unprotected laptop was stolen** from a hotel. The thief **accessed confidential documents** because the device wasn't encrypted.

Lesson: Lost or stolen devices should never expose sensitive data—always enable encryption.

C. Strong Authentication and Password Security

Using **strong passwords and multi-factor authentication (MFA)** prevents unauthorized access to remote work accounts.

☑ **Essential Password & Authentication Tips:**
✔ Use **a password manager** to generate and store unique passwords.
✔ Enable **Multi-Factor Authentication (MFA)** for all work-related accounts.
✔ Use **biometric authentication** (Face ID, fingerprint login) for devices.
✔ Change passwords **immediately after a suspected breach**.

195

Example:
A remote IT consultant **used the same weak password** for Slack and email. When their credentials leaked in a **data breach**, hackers took over both accounts.

Lesson: A compromised password can lead to full account takeovers—use MFA everywhere.

D. Safe Cloud Storage & File Sharing

Cloud storage is essential for remote work, but **improper file-sharing** can expose sensitive company data.

☑ **How to Secure Cloud Storage & File Sharing:**
✔ Use **company-approved cloud services** (Google Drive, OneDrive, Dropbox).
✔ **Enable encryption** for sensitive files.
✔ Restrict **file sharing permissions** to specific people.
✔ Avoid **publicly accessible links** (anyone with the link can access your data).

 Example:
A freelancer **accidentally shared a Google Drive folder** with public access. Competitors **downloaded confidential project details** before they noticed.

Lesson: Always review sharing permissions before sending cloud storage links.

3. Real-World Attack: A Compromised Remote Worker's Device

Case Study: How a Remote Worker Caused a Major Data Breach

Scenario:

A **software developer working remotely** for a large company **logged into their work account from a café Wi-Fi network**.

How the Attack Happened:

①The developer connected to **"CoffeeShop_FreeWiFi"**, not realizing it was a **rogue network set up by hackers**. ②Hackers **intercepted their login credentials** and used them to access **company databases**. ③**Malware was planted** on company systems, leading to a **data breach of 1.2 million customer records**. ④The company **lost millions in fines and legal fees** due to leaked personal data.

How This Could Have Been Prevented:

☑ **Using a VPN** would have encrypted their internet connection, preventing credential theft.
☑ **Enabling MFA** would have blocked unauthorized logins.
☑ **Avoiding public Wi-Fi** without security measures would have mitigated the risk.

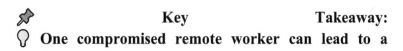
📌 Key Takeaway:
💡 **One compromised remote worker can lead to a**

massive corporate breach. Security policies must be followed at all times.

---

4. Summary: How to Work Securely from Anywhere

☑ Remote Work Cybersecurity Checklist

✔ **Use a VPN** when working from public Wi-Fi.

✔ **Secure personal devices** (encryption, antivirus, remote wipe).

✔ **Enable Multi-Factor Authentication (MFA)** on all accounts.

✔ **Use a password manager** to create strong, unique passwords.

✔ **Update software regularly** to patch vulnerabilities.

✔ **Be cautious with cloud file sharing** (never use public links).

✔ **Avoid phishing emails**—verify all login requests.

✔ **Always log out of work accounts** on shared or public devices.

📌 **Final Thought:**
💡 Remote work offers freedom, but also risk—protect your devices, data, and credentials at all times.

Next Chapter: Cybersecurity for Smart Homes –
Protecting IoT Devices from Hackers

In **Chapter 22**, we'll explore how to **secure smart home devices, IoT security risks, and how hackers exploit connected technology**.

⌂ **Your smart home might be spying on you—let's secure it!**

CHAPTER 22

The Rise of Ransomware and Cyber Extortion

Introduction

Ransomware and cyber extortion have **emerged as some of the most financially damaging cyber threats** of the modern era. In **2021 alone, the global cost of ransomware attacks exceeded $20 billion**.

Cybercriminals are increasingly using **ransomware** not only to encrypt data but also to **threaten public exposure** of sensitive information if their demands are not met. **Extortion is becoming a profitable and low-risk business for hackers.**

Why Ransomware and Cyber Extortion Matter

✔ **Ransomware attacks are escalating** in both frequency and   sophistication.
✔ **Cyber extortion** exploits businesses' fear of **reputational   damage   and   data   loss**.
✔ **Every sector is at risk**, but **healthcare, education, and government** organizations are particularly vulnerable.

In this chapter, we'll explore:

- **How ransomware works and why it's so dangerous** – The inner workings of a ransomware attack.
- **The evolution of cyber extortion tactics** – How criminals have adapted their methods.

- **Case study: A hospital taken hostage by ransomware** – A real-world example of ransomware's devastating impact.

By the end of this chapter, you'll understand the **rising threat of ransomware and extortion**, and how businesses can **protect themselves from these evolving dangers**.

---

1. How Ransomware Works and Why It's So Dangerous

A. What is Ransomware?

Ransomware is a type of **malware** that encrypts a victim's files, rendering them **unusable** until a **ransom** is paid. Ransomware attacks often involve a demand for **cryptocurrency payments**—which are difficult to trace—making it a **preferred method for cybercriminals**.

B. The Stages of a Ransomware Attack

1 **Infection** – Ransomware usually infiltrates systems via **phishing emails, malicious websites**, or **exploited software vulnerabilities**.
2 **Encryption** – Once inside, ransomware encrypts **files, databases, and backups**, often with strong encryption algorithms.
3 **Ransom Demand** – Victims are presented with a **ransom note**, demanding payment in exchange for the decryption key.
4 **Decryption (or Not)** – If the ransom is paid, the attacker may or may not provide a **working decryption key**. In many cases, the victim is left **without the key**, and the attacker may demand more money.

📌 **Key Takeaway: Ransomware works by holding critical data hostage until the victim pays a ransom— often with no guarantee of recovery.**

C. Why Ransomware is So Dangerous

✅ **Targets High-Value Data** – Ransomware typically targets **sensitive data** in industries like healthcare, finance, and   government.

✅ **Denial of Service** – Ransomware **cripples operations**, making critical services or data **inaccessible**, often for days or   weeks.

✅ **Costly Impact** – The **costs of recovery** (ransom payment, legal fees, business downtime) can reach **millions**.

✅ **Reputation Damage** – Data breaches associated with ransomware can **severely damage an organization's reputation**, leading to **customer distrust**.

📌   **Example:**
In **2017**, the **WannaCry ransomware** attack affected more than **200,000 computers across 150 countries**, crippling industries like healthcare and manufacturing, and demanding **Bitcoin payments**.

Lesson: Ransomware has the potential to bring entire organizations to a halt—businesses must prepare for such attacks.

2. The Evolution of Cyber Extortion Tactics

A. From Ransomware to Double and Triple Extortion

Cyber extortion has **evolved significantly** over the years, with attackers now **leveraging multiple tactics** to maximize profits.

☑ **Double Extortion** – After encrypting files, attackers threaten to **publish stolen data** if the ransom isn't paid. This tactic preys on victims' **fear of reputational damage**.
☑ **Triple Extortion** – The latest form of cyber extortion, where attackers **target the victim's customers, partners, or employees**, demanding ransoms from **multiple parties** to get the data back.

📌   **Example:**
In 2020, the **Maze ransomware group** began using **double extortion**, leaking sensitive corporate data to the public if the company refused to pay the ransom.

Lesson: Ransomware attacks are becoming more aggressive, with cybercriminals targeting not just the company but also their clients and customers.

B. Ransomware as a Service (RaaS)

With the rise of **Ransomware-as-a-Service (RaaS)** platforms, **anyone can become a ransomware attacker**, even without technical expertise. These platforms allow **affiliates** to pay for **access to ransomware tools** and **share profits** with the developers.

📌 **Example:**
The **REvil ransomware group** operates a **RaaS model**, allowing anyone to use their **ransomware tools** to target victims. They receive a **cut of the ransom** while the developers maintain the ransomware infrastructure.

Lesson: Ransomware is no longer the work of lone hackers—cybercrime is now an industry.

---

3. Case Study: A Hospital Taken Hostage by Ransomware

The Attack:

In **2020**, a **ransomware attack hit the University of Vermont Medical Center (UVM)**. The attackers encrypted **critical hospital data** and demanded a **large ransom** in Bitcoin to decrypt it.

The Timeline of the Attack:

1. **Infection** – The hospital's network was infected with **Netwalker ransomware** via a **phishing email**.
2. **Encryption** – Files, including **patient records, imaging data, and hospital systems**, were encrypted and rendered **unusable**.
3. **Ransom Demand** – Attackers demanded **$10 million** in Bitcoin for the decryption key.
4. **Operations Halted** – The hospital's **critical services, including scheduling and medical imaging**, were severely disrupted.
5. **Recovery** – While the hospital didn't pay the ransom, the

recovery **process** took **several weeks**, resulting in significant operational downtime.

📌 Key Impact:

- **Delayed medical procedures** and treatment, jeopardizing patient care.
- Loss of **trust** from patients and healthcare professionals.
- **$2 million** in costs for recovery and **rebuilding systems**.

How the Hospital Responded:

- **Crisis communication** – The hospital **informed patients** about delays and provided regular updates.
- **Strengthened defenses** – After recovery, the hospital **implemented more robust security measures**, including **MFA, network segmentation, and advanced threat detection**.

Lesson: Ransomware can have devastating effects on critical infrastructure, especially in healthcare, where lives are at stake.

---

4. How to Protect Against Ransomware and Cyber Extortion

To protect your business or organization from **ransomware and extortion**, follow these key steps:

✅ Best Practices for Ransomware Protection

✔ **Regular Backups** – Regularly back up critical data and **store it offline**. Ensure backups are **tested** for integrity.

✔ **Patch Vulnerabilities** – Apply security patches to software and systems as soon as they're available.

✔ **Network Segmentation** – Divide your network into isolated segments to **contain ransomware** if it spreads.

✔ **User Training** – Conduct regular **phishing awareness training** to prevent malware from entering through email.

✔ **Multi-Factor Authentication (MFA)** – Enforce MFA on **critical accounts** to prevent unauthorized access.

✔ **Incident Response Plan** – Have a detailed incident response plan to quickly **contain and recover** from an attack.

✔ **Cyber Insurance** – Consider cyber insurance to mitigate the **financial impact** of a ransomware attack.

📌 **Example:**
A global manufacturer used **advanced endpoint protection**, **network segmentation**, and **employee training** to stop a **ransomware attack** before it spread across its systems.

Lesson: A comprehensive defense strategy—combining security, training, and backup systems—is the best way to prevent and recover from ransomware attacks.

Key Takeaways

✔ **Ransomware works by encrypting data and demanding ransom for its release**—often with no guarantee that the attacker will honor the deal.

✔ **Double and triple extortion tactics** are becoming more common, with hackers targeting customers and clients in addition to businesses.

✔ **Ransomware-as-a-Service (RaaS)** allows anyone to

launch an attack, making ransomware even more widespread.

✔ **The UVM ransomware attack** shows the devastating impact on healthcare systems, emphasizing the importance of cybersecurity in critical infrastructure.

✔ **Regular backups, network segmentation, and strong security practices** are essential to protect against ransomware and cyber extortion.

Next Chapter: Cybersecurity for Digital Transformation – Securing Cloud Environments

In **Chapter 23**, we'll explore how to **secure cloud environments** and protect **critical data** as more businesses transition to the cloud.

☁ **The future is in the cloud—but how do we secure it? Let's dive in!**

CHAPTER 23

The Dark Web and Cybercrime Economy

Introduction

The **Dark Web** is often portrayed as the hidden, criminal underbelly of the internet, where **illegal activities** flourish. While the Dark Web itself is simply a **part of the deep web**—a portion of the internet not indexed by search engines—its **anonymity and encryption features** have made it a haven for **cybercriminals**.

On the Dark Web, **stolen data, hacking tools, and malicious services** are sold to the highest bidder, fueling the **cybercrime economy**. With the rise of **Ransomware-as-a-Service (RaaS)** and **data breaches**, the Dark Web has become an **unregulated marketplace** for **illicit activity**.

Why the Dark Web Matters

✔ **Stolen data is sold in bulk**, allowing cybercriminals to engage in **fraud, identity theft**, and **extortion**.
✔ **Cybercrime services** on the Dark Web provide tools and expertise for **carrying out attacks** (e.g., phishing, malware distribution, DDoS).
✔ **Hackers and criminals exploit anonymity** to evade detection, making **investigations difficult** for law enforcement.

In this chapter, we will explore:

- **What the Dark Web is and how it works** – Understanding this hidden corner of the internet.
- **Black markets for stolen data and hacking services** – How criminal activity is organized and profited.
- **Real-world cases of cybercrime on the Dark Web** – Case studies that show the impact of Dark Web activity.

By the end of this chapter, you'll understand the **role of the Dark Web in the cybercrime economy** and how businesses and individuals can **protect themselves from Dark Web threats**.

1. What is the Dark Web, and How Does it Work?

The **Dark Web** is a **small, hidden portion** of the internet that is intentionally **hidden from search engines** and requires special software (like **Tor** or **I2P**) to access it.

A. How the Dark Web Works

1. **Anonymity** – The Dark Web allows users to **conceal their identities** through **end-to-end encryption** and **proxy servers**, making it hard to trace activities.
2. **Accessing the Dark Web** – To visit the Dark Web, users need special **browser software** like **Tor (The Onion Router)**, which routes traffic through multiple layers of encryption, hiding the user's location and identity.
3. **Onion Domains** – Websites on the Dark Web typically use .onion domains, which are only accessible via Tor, ensuring **privacy and anonymity**.

🚀 **Key Takeaway:** The **Dark Web** is a part of the **Deep Web** that is intentionally hidden and encrypted, providing **complete anonymity** for users and sites.

209

B. Dark Web vs. Deep Web vs. Surface Web

Web Type	Description	Access
Surface Web	The part of the internet **accessible by traditional browsers** (Google, Bing, etc.).	Easily accessible to everyone.
Deep Web	All parts of the web not indexed by traditional search engines (e.g., private databases, academic resources).	Accessible with proper credentials or access.
Dark Web	A small section of the Deep Web where **anonymous activity** takes place, often for illegal purposes.	Requires specialized software like Tor to access.

📌 **Example:**
The **Deep Web** includes resources like **private company databases**, which are not meant for public access. The **Dark Web**, in contrast, is often a marketplace for illicit items and services.

2. Black Markets for Stolen Data and Hacking Services

On the Dark Web, cybercriminals sell everything from **stolen login credentials** to **sophisticated hacking tools**, creating a thriving **cybercrime economy**.

210

A. Black Markets for Stolen Data

Stolen data is one of the most lucrative commodities on the Dark Web. Hackers often steal **personal information** during data breaches and sell it to the highest bidder.

Stolen Data Type	How It's Used	Example
Personal Identifiable Information (PII)	Used for **identity theft**, credit fraud, and phishing scams.	Stolen **Social Security numbers** used to open fake accounts.
Credit Card Information	Sold for **fraudulent transactions**.	**500,000 stolen credit card numbers** are sold for $1 each.
Login Credentials	Used for **credential stuffing attacks** on various websites.	Leaked **email and password lists** used to hack into email accounts.
Medical Data	**Resold on the Dark Web** for insurance fraud or **blackmailing victims**.	Stolen **patient records** are sold for identity theft or fraudulent medical claims.

🔖 **Example:** In **2018**, the **Collection #1** data breach exposed **773 million email addresses and passwords**, which were sold on the Dark Web and used in credential stuffing attacks.

B. Hacking Services on the Dark Web

Cybercriminals often **rent out hacking tools** or **offer "as-a-service" options**, allowing anyone with sufficient funds to launch attacks.

✅ Popular Hacking Services on the Dark Web:

Service	How It Works	Example
Ransomware-as-a-Service (RaaS)	Hackers provide **ransomware tools** to affiliates, who can launch attacks in exchange for a share of the ransom.	**REvil ransomware** offers **easy-to-use ransomware tools** for anyone to launch attacks.
DDoS-for-Hire	Attackers rent out **botnets** to flood websites with traffic, rendering them unusable.	**Stresser services** offer DDoS attacks for as little as **$5 for 10 minutes**.
Phishing Kits	Pre-made tools that facilitate **email phishing campaigns** to steal credentials or infect victims.	Hackers sell **customizable phishing email templates** and malicious attachments.
Exploit Kits	These tools automate the **exploitation of software vulnerabilities** to gain	Kits that exploit **unpatched Flash vulnerabilities** to inject malware into victims' systems.

Service	How It Works	Example
	unauthorized access to systems.	

📌 **Example:** The **NetWalker ransomware group rented out its ransomware** to affiliates, leading to a **spike in ransomware attacks** across various sectors in 2020.

3. Real-World Cases of Cybercrime on the Dark Web

A. Case Study: The 2017 Equifax Data Breach

Overview:

In **2017**, **Equifax**, one of the largest credit reporting agencies, suffered a massive **data breach**, exposing **147 million individuals' personal data**—including **names, Social Security numbers, birth dates, and addresses**.

How the Dark Web Was Used:

1️⃣ **The data was sold** on the Dark Web shortly after the breach, making it easily accessible to hackers. 2️⃣ **Cybercriminals used the stolen data** for **identity theft, opening fraudulent credit accounts, and insurance fraud**. 3️⃣ The breach led to **fines** and a **class action lawsuit**.

📌 **Lesson:** The **Equifax breach** highlights the importance of **data**

protection and **early breach detection**. The stolen data on the Dark Web **enabled massive identity theft** and **fraud**.

B. Case Study: The 2020 Twitter Hack

In **2020**, a **high-profile Twitter hack** occurred when attackers **compromised multiple high-profile accounts** (e.g., Elon Musk, Barack Obama) to promote a **Bitcoin scam**.

How the Dark Web Was Used:

1 **The attackers gained access** through a **social engineering attack** targeting Twitter employees.
2 Once in, the hackers **took control of verified accounts**, using them to post fraudulent **Bitcoin donation requests**.
3 The attack was **coordinated and executed** with **tools** likely sourced from the Dark Web.

📌 **Lesson:** **Social engineering** combined with **Dark Web tools** can lead to devastating attacks on **high-profile targets**.

---

4. How to Protect Yourself from the Dark Web Threats

Protecting yourself and your organization from **Dark Web threats** requires proactive security measures.

✅ **Best Practices for Protection:**

✔️ **Monitor your data on the Dark Web** – Use services like **Have I Been Pwned** to check if your personal data is exposed.

✔️ **Enable MFA** on all accounts to prevent unauthorized logins.

✔️ **Encrypt sensitive information** both in storage and transit.

✔️ **Regularly update software and patch vulnerabilities** to prevent exploitation.

✔️ **Limit data shared online** – Be cautious about sharing personal information on social media.

✔️ **Monitor financial statements** for suspicious activity or fraud.

 Example: A global retailer **implemented Dark Web monitoring** for **stolen payment data**. Upon finding breached data, they notified affected customers and **blocked compromised credit cards** before fraud occurred.

Key Takeaways

✔️ **The Dark Web** is a hidden part of the internet where **cybercriminals engage in illegal activities** like selling stolen data and offering hacking services.

✔️ **Black markets on the Dark Web** are a **major hub for cybercrime**, with stolen data and ransomware services being sold for profit.

✔️ **Real-world cases** like the **Equifax breach** and **Twitter hack** show the devastating impact of the Dark Web on **personal security and corporate operations**.

✔️ **Proactive monitoring, data encryption, and strong**

authentication are essential to protect yourself and your organization from Dark Web threats.

Next Chapter: The Future of Cybersecurity – AI, Quantum Computing, and Beyond

In **Chapter 24**, we'll dive into the **cutting-edge technologies** shaping the future of cybersecurity, including **artificial intelligence, machine learning**, and **quantum computing**.

🚀 **The future of cybersecurity is fast approaching—let's explore what's next!**

CHAPTER 24

Cybersecurity in the Age of IoT and Smart Devices

Introduction

The rise of **Internet of Things (IoT) devices** and **smart home technology** has dramatically changed how we live, work, and interact with the world. From **smart thermostats** and **security cameras** to **wearables** and **voice assistants**, these devices offer **convenience** and **connectivity**. However, they also pose significant **security risks**.

The **vast number of connected devices**—often lacking proper security protocols—creates an expanding attack surface for cybercriminals. Vulnerabilities in these devices can be exploited by hackers to **gain unauthorized access**, **steal data**, or even **compromise entire networks**.

Why IoT and Smart Devices Matter for Cybersecurity

✔ **Billions of connected devices** create more opportunities for cybercriminals to launch attacks.
✔ **Weak or no security measures** on many IoT devices leave them open to exploitation.
✔ **IoT vulnerabilities** can be used to gain access to broader home or organizational networks.

In this chapter, we'll explore:

- **Why smart devices are a security risk** – Understanding the inherent vulnerabilities in IoT.
- **How attackers exploit vulnerabilities in IoT devices** – Methods used to compromise smart devices.
- **Case study: A hacked smart home device** – A real-world example of how vulnerable devices can be exploited.

By the end of this chapter, you'll understand how to **secure your smart devices** and protect your **digital ecosystem** from IoT-based threats.

---

1. Why Smart Devices Are a Security Risk

A. The Expanding Attack Surface

With the proliferation of **smart home gadgets, wearable tech, and connected office devices**, there are now **billions of IoT devices** in use worldwide. Many of these devices are **poorly secured** or lack **basic cybersecurity features**, making them easy targets for attackers.

Why Smart Devices Are Vulnerable:

1 **Default Passwords** – Many devices come with **easy-to-guess default passwords** that users fail to change.
2 **Insecure Communication** – IoT devices often use **unsecured protocols** (e.g., HTTP instead of HTTPS), making it easy for attackers to intercept data.
3 **Lack of Updates** – Many IoT manufacturers **don't provide regular software updates**, leaving devices vulnerable to known exploits.
4 **Limited Device Security** – Most IoT devices are designed for **functionality** and **convenience**, not security.

218

📌 **Example:**
In **2016**, the **Mirai botnet** was created using **thousands of insecure IoT devices** (cameras, routers, DVRs). This botnet launched one of the **largest DDoS attacks** in history, overwhelming major websites like **Twitter, Netflix, and Reddit**.

Lesson: The more connected devices you have, the greater your risk. Insecure IoT devices can serve as entry points for cybercriminals.

B. The Role of IoT in Everyday Life

Smart devices are **integrated into our daily routines**, making them **critical parts of home and work ecosystems**. This includes:

- **Smart homes** (thermostats, lights, security cameras, appliances)
- **Wearable devices** (fitness trackers, health monitors)
- **Connected vehicles** (car systems that allow remote diagnostics and control)
- **Healthcare IoT** (medical devices that send real-time data to doctors)
- **Smart office devices** (printers, thermostats, smart locks)

While these devices provide **convenience**, they also create **significant attack vectors** if not secured properly.

📌 **Key Takeaway:** Smart devices are **convenient**, but without proper security measures, they can become **attack points** for hackers.

2. How Attackers Exploit Vulnerabilities in IoT Devices

A. Common IoT Vulnerabilities

Cybercriminals take advantage of **known vulnerabilities** in IoT devices to gain access to networks, steal data, or cause damage. These vulnerabilities can arise from design flaws, poor configurations, or lack of updates.

Common Attack Techniques:

1 **Device Hijacking** – Attackers take control of IoT devices, turning them into **botnets** or **data-stealing agents**.
2 **Man-in-the-Middle (MitM) Attacks** – Attackers intercept unencrypted communication between IoT devices and servers.
3 **Denial of Service (DoS) Attacks** – Attackers overload IoT devices with traffic, causing them to **malfunction** or **shut down**.
4 **Unauthorized Access** – Attackers exploit weak passwords, default credentials, or poor access control to **gain control over devices**.
5 **Firmware Exploits** – Vulnerabilities in device firmware (software that controls the hardware) can allow attackers to **install malicious code**.

📌 **Example:**
In 2019, a smart camera manufacturer found that their devices were vulnerable to remote exploits because **the default password was never changed** by users. Hackers **took control of the cameras**, causing massive privacy breaches.

Lesson: Weak security in IoT devices can lead to unauthorized access, stolen data, and compromised networks.

B. IoT Botnets and DDoS Attacks

One of the most damaging outcomes of insecure IoT devices is their **involvement in botnets**, which are networks of **compromised devices** used to launch **Distributed Denial of Service (DDoS) attacks**. These attacks overwhelm a website or service with **massive amounts of traffic**, rendering it unusable.

The Role of IoT in Botnets:

- **IoT devices** (e.g., routers, cameras, DVRs) are often **left unprotected** with weak passwords, making them **easy targets**.
- Attackers can take control of these devices and use them to launch **massive-scale DDoS attacks**, without the device owner's knowledge.

🔖 **Example:**
The **2016 Mirai botnet** attack leveraged over **600,000 IoT devices**—including **IP cameras, routers, and DVRs**—to take down major websites and services.

Lesson: Insecure IoT devices can be hijacked and used in massive DDoS attacks that cause widespread disruption.

3. Case Study: A Hacked Smart Home Device

Scenario:

A **family's smart home security camera** was hacked, giving cybercriminals access to private footage.

How the Attack Happened:

1. **Insecure Camera Setup** – The family **installed a smart security camera** in their home but **failed to change the default password**.
2. **Unauthorized Access** – A hacker scanned for **unprotected IoT devices** with default credentials. They **found the camera** and gained access to live footage.
3. **Exploitation** – The hacker used the camera's **audio capabilities** to **listen in** on private conversations and gather sensitive information.
4. **Ransom Demand** – The hacker **demanded a ransom** to delete the footage, threatening to release it online if their demands weren't met.

How This Could Have Been Prevented:

☑ **Change default passwords** on all IoT devices during setup.

☑ **Enable encryption** for communication between IoT devices and servers.

☑ **Use a firewall** or **network segmentation** to isolate IoT devices from critical systems.

☑ **Regularly update firmware** and software on all connected devices.

📌 **Key Takeaway:** **Default passwords** and **lack of encryption** are common vulnerabilities in IoT devices. Hackers exploit these weaknesses to gain unauthorized access and potentially use the devices for malicious purposes.

---

4. How to Secure Your IoT Devices

Protecting your IoT devices requires **strong security measures** to prevent exploitation. Follow these steps to enhance the security of your connected devices:

✅ IoT Security Best Practices:

✔ **Change default passwords** – Always set a **unique, strong password** for your devices.

✔ **Enable encryption** – Use **encrypted communication** protocols like **HTTPS** to protect data.

✔ **Use a separate network** – Isolate IoT devices from your primary network by creating a **guest Wi-Fi network**.

✔ **Regularly update firmware** – Apply **security patches** and updates to your IoT devices as soon as they're available.

✔ **Monitor device activity** – Use **device management software** to track device behavior and flag any unusual activity.

✔ **Disable unused features** – Turn off any unnecessary features, such as **remote access**, when not in use.

✔ **Use firewalls and endpoint protection** – Install firewalls and security software to protect devices from external threats.

223

📌 **Example:**
A **homeowner implemented network segmentation** between their smart home devices and the rest of their household devices. As a result, even if one device was compromised, it couldn't affect the rest of the network.

Lesson: Taking proactive steps to secure IoT devices can significantly reduce the risk of cyberattacks.

Key Takeaways

✔ **IoT devices are highly vulnerable** to cyberattacks, especially when **default passwords** and **unsecured communication** are used.
✔ Attackers can exploit these vulnerabilities to gain access to personal data, launch DDoS attacks, or **steal sensitive information**.
✔ **Best practices** like **changing passwords, enabling encryption**, and **regularly updating firmware** are essential to securing IoT devices.
✔ **Network segmentation** and **firewalls** can help isolate vulnerable devices from critical systems.

Next Chapter: Cybersecurity in the Future — AI, Quantum Computing, and Beyond

In **Chapter 25**, we'll explore the **cutting-edge technologies** reshaping cybersecurity, including **AI-driven defenses, quantum computing**, and the next wave of **cyber threats**.

🚀 **The future of cybersecurity is here—let's dive into the emerging trends!**

CHAPTER 25

Blockchain and Cybersecurity: A New Frontier

Introduction

Blockchain technology has revolutionized various industries, offering unprecedented levels of **decentralization, transparency, and immutability**. Its use in **cryptocurrencies** like Bitcoin has attracted global attention, but **blockchain's potential** goes far beyond financial transactions.

As cybersecurity challenges continue to evolve, **blockchain is emerging as a powerful tool** for securing systems, protecting data integrity, and reducing vulnerabilities. However, **blockchain security** itself is not without flaws, and new **vulnerabilities** and **threats** have emerged as the technology matures.

Why Blockchain Matters for Cybersecurity

✔ **Decentralization** means no central point of failure, making it harder for cybercriminals to compromise data.
✔ **Immutability** ensures that once data is written to the blockchain, it **cannot be altered** or deleted.
✔ **Smart contracts** can automate security processes and reduce the need for intermediaries, leading to **fewer attack vectors**.

In this chapter, we'll explore:

- **How blockchain can be used for cybersecurity** – The advantages and innovative uses of blockchain in securing systems.
- **Blockchain security threats and vulnerabilities** – The risks that blockchain faces as it continues to gain traction.
- **Real-world blockchain hacks and what we learned** – Case studies that highlight the security risks and lessons learned from blockchain-related cyber incidents.

By the end of this chapter, you'll understand **how blockchain can be a game-changer in cybersecurity**, but also how its **unique vulnerabilities** require careful consideration in its adoption.

---

1. How Blockchain Can Be Used for Cybersecurity

A. Decentralized Identity Management

One of the most promising uses of blockchain in cybersecurity is **identity management**. In traditional systems, a **centralized database** stores personal information, which can be a target for hackers. Blockchain, by contrast, allows individuals to have **control over their own identity** through **decentralized identity solutions**.

✅ How It Works:

- Blockchain stores **hashed versions** of personal data, ensuring that **sensitive information** is not exposed.
- **Decentralized identifiers (DIDs)** allow users to verify their identity without relying on a central authority.
- Blockchain's **immutability** ensures that once identity data is recorded, it **cannot be altered or tampered with**.

📌 **Example:**
Microsoft is implementing blockchain for **self-sovereign identity** systems, enabling individuals to control and verify their own digital identities without relying on central authorities.

Lesson: Blockchain's decentralized approach can provide more secure and privacy-respecting identity management systems.

B. Secure Transactions and Smart Contracts

Blockchain's ability to ensure **secure transactions** is at the core of its value in cybersecurity. With **cryptographic techniques** and **distributed ledgers**, blockchain can provide **a tamper-resistant record** of transactions, which is ideal for industries such as **finance, supply chain, and healthcare**.

How Smart Contracts Enhance Security:

- **Smart contracts** are self-executing contracts with the terms of the agreement directly written into code.
- Blockchain ensures that **smart contracts** are executed only when certain conditions are met, and once the contract is executed, it is recorded on the blockchain and cannot be altered.
- These contracts remove the need for **third-party intermediaries**, **reducing human error** and making transactions more secure.

📌 **Example:**
In **supply chain management**, blockchain is used to track and verify **every transaction** in the supply chain, from raw

materials to the final product. This ensures that products are not tampered with and that all steps are verified, enhancing transparency and security.

Lesson: Blockchain-based smart contracts and transactions provide a high level of security by automating processes and removing intermediaries.

C. Blockchain for Data Integrity and Anti-Tampering

Blockchain's inherent feature of **immutability** makes it ideal for maintaining **data integrity**. Once data is recorded on a blockchain, it becomes nearly impossible to alter or delete it without detection.

How Blockchain Ensures Data Integrity:

- **Every block** in the blockchain contains a **cryptographic hash** of the previous block, forming a chain that is incredibly difficult to alter.
- When changes are attempted, the **entire blockchain** must be modified, which is computationally infeasible for attackers due to the decentralized nature of the network.

📌   **Example:**
Healthcare providers are increasingly using blockchain to store and share patient records securely. Blockchain guarantees that patient data is **tamper-proof** and only accessible to authorized users, ensuring **data integrity**.

Lesson: Blockchain's immutability and transparency can protect data from tampering and ensure its authenticity.

2. Blockchain Security Threats and Vulnerabilities

While blockchain is known for its security features, it is not immune to **attacks and vulnerabilities**. As blockchain technology grows and evolves, so too do the tactics and strategies used by cybercriminals.

A. 51% Attack

In a **51% attack**, an attacker or group of attackers gains control of more than 50% of the **mining power** or **hashrate** in a blockchain network, allowing them to manipulate transactions.

✅ Impact:

- The attacker can **reverse transactions, double-spend coins**, or **prevent new transactions from being added** to the blockchain.
- This type of attack is particularly dangerous on **smaller or newer blockchain networks** that don't have a large enough base of miners to prevent such an attack.

📌 **Example:**
In 2018, the **Bitcoin Gold** network suffered a **51% attack**, where hackers manipulated the blockchain to **double-spend coins**, resulting in a loss of **$18 million**.

Lesson: While blockchain offers secure data storage, smaller networks may be vulnerable to attacks if not properly decentralized.

B. Smart Contract Vulnerabilities

Smart contracts, while powerful, can introduce their own security issues. Bugs, poor coding, and improper testing can lead to serious vulnerabilities.

Common Smart Contract Vulnerabilities:

1 **Reentrancy Attacks** – This happens when a contract calls an external function before updating its state, allowing attackers to **withdraw more funds** than intended. 2 **Integer Overflow/Underflow** – Smart contracts that don't properly handle large numbers can lead to **unexpected behavior** in the contract's logic, causing financial loss or unintended consequences. 3 **Lack of Access Control** – If smart contracts don't properly restrict access to certain functions, attackers may gain **unauthorized control** over funds or assets.

📌 **Example:** The **DAO Hack** in 2016 exploited a **reentrancy vulnerability** in a smart contract, allowing attackers to drain **$50 million** worth of Ethereum from the contract.

Lesson: Smart contract vulnerabilities are a significant risk—thorough auditing and secure coding practices are essential.

C. Blockchain-Related Privacy Issues

While blockchain's transparency offers benefits, it can also pose **privacy concerns**. Data on the blockchain is **publicly**

available for anyone to inspect, which could expose **sensitive personal information** if not handled correctly.

☑ **Solutions:**

- **Private Blockchains** – These offer restricted access to information, ensuring only authorized parties can view sensitive data.
- **Zero-Knowledge Proofs** – A cryptographic method that allows data to be verified without revealing the actual data itself.

📌 **Example:**

The **ZCash** blockchain utilizes **zero-knowledge proofs** to ensure the privacy of financial transactions, while still maintaining the security of the blockchain.

Lesson: While transparency is a key feature of blockchain, privacy-enhancing technologies must be employed to protect sensitive data.

---

3. Real-World Blockchain Hacks and What We Learned

A. The DAO Hack (2016)

What Happened:

The **DAO (Decentralized Autonomous Organization)** was a venture fund running on the Ethereum blockchain. Attackers exploited a vulnerability in the DAO's smart contract to **drain funds**—resulting in a loss of **$50 million**.

Lessons Learned:

- **Smart contracts must be thoroughly audited** before deployment.
- Blockchain doesn't eliminate the need for **secure coding practices** and **comprehensive testing**.

B. Bitfinex Hack (2016)

What Happened:

In 2016, the **Bitfinex** cryptocurrency exchange was hacked, resulting in the theft of **120,000 Bitcoins** worth around **$72 million** at the time. Despite blockchain's immutability, the attack targeted **user wallets** and the platform's weak security measures.

Lessons Learned:

- **Exchanges and wallets must implement robust security practices** such as **multi-signature wallets** and **cold storage**.
- Blockchain-based theft is still possible if **third-party systems** (like exchanges) are compromised.

4. How to Protect Against Blockchain Security Risks

To fully leverage the benefits of blockchain technology while minimizing risks, businesses and individuals must take proactive steps:

✅ Blockchain Security Best Practices:

✔ **Conduct regular security audits** of blockchain networks and smart contracts.
✔ **Use multi-signature wallets** for securing assets.
✔ **Implement privacy-enhancing solutions** like zero-knowledge proofs for sensitive data.
✔ **Monitor for unusual activity** in blockchain networks and smart contracts.
✔ **Keep software updated** to protect against known vulnerabilities and exploits.

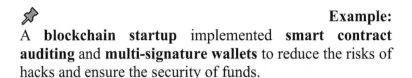 **Example:** A **blockchain startup** implemented **smart contract auditing** and **multi-signature wallets** to reduce the risks of hacks and ensure the security of funds.

Lesson: Blockchain can significantly improve security, but only when implemented with careful attention to security protocols.

Key Takeaways

✔ **Blockchain offers significant benefits** for cybersecurity, particularly in identity management, data integrity, and secure transactions.
✔ **Smart contracts** and decentralized systems need **thorough audits** and **secure coding practices** to avoid vulnerabilities.
✔ **Blockchain-related security issues**, including **51% attacks, privacy concerns,** and **smart contract vulnerabilities**, need to be actively mitigated.
✔ **Real-world hacks**, like **the DAO hack** and **Bitfinex**

breach, show that blockchain systems are not invulnerable and must be protected with **best practices**.

Next Chapter: The Future of Cybersecurity – AI, Quantum Computing, and Beyond

In **Chapter 26**, we'll explore how **artificial intelligence, quantum computing,** and other **emerging technologies** will reshape the future of cybersecurity.

🚀 **The next wave of cybersecurity is on the horizon— let's see what's coming!**

CHAPTER 26

Cybersecurity Careers and How to Get Started

Introduction

As cyber threats continue to grow in sophistication and scale, the demand for **cybersecurity professionals** is higher than ever. Companies across industries are investing in **top-tier security talent** to protect their critical data and systems from malicious actors. Whether you're just starting out or looking to pivot your career, cybersecurity offers numerous **opportunities** for individuals who are passionate about technology and protecting the digital world.

In this chapter, we'll explore:

- **Career paths** in cybersecurity, from penetration testing to security engineering.
- The **certifications** that can help you break into the field and grow your career.
- **How to build hands-on skills** and create a **cybersecurity portfolio** that stands out to employers.

By the end of this chapter, you'll understand the **different cybersecurity roles**, how to pursue a career in this field, and the **practical steps** you can take to launch your cybersecurity career.

1. Career Paths in Cybersecurity

Cybersecurity is a broad field, with numerous specializations and career paths. Whether you're interested in **offensive security**, **defensive security**, or **risk management**, there are opportunities in each area.

A. Penetration Tester (Ethical Hacker)

Penetration testers, also known as **ethical hackers**, are hired to test the security of systems by attempting to **break into** them in a controlled, authorized manner. They identify weaknesses in systems, networks, and applications and provide recommendations to improve security.

Key Responsibilities:

- Conducting **penetration tests** on networks, applications, and systems.
- Identifying and exploiting **vulnerabilities**.
- Writing detailed reports of findings and providing **recommendations for mitigation**.

📌 Skills Required:

- Strong understanding of **network protocols**, operating systems, and security tools.
- Familiarity with tools like **Metasploit, Burp Suite, and Kali Linux**.
- Excellent knowledge of **ethical hacking techniques** and **vulnerability assessment**.

B. Security Operations Center (SOC) Analyst

SOC analysts work in **security operations centers**, where they monitor and respond to potential security incidents. They use a combination of tools and techniques to **identify, analyze, and mitigate** security threats in real-time.

Key Responsibilities:

- **Monitoring security alerts** for signs of attacks (e.g., DDoS, malware).
- Analyzing system logs and network traffic for **indicators of compromise (IOCs)**.
- Escalating issues to the **incident response team** for further action.

📌 Skills Required:

- Experience with **SIEM (Security Information and Event Management)** tools like **Splunk** or **IBM QRadar**.
- Knowledge of **network security protocols** and experience in **incident handling**.
- Understanding of **malware analysis** and basic **forensics**.

C. Security Engineer

Security engineers are responsible for building and maintaining **secure infrastructures**. They design, implement, and configure security tools and systems to protect the organization's networks and applications from attacks.

Key Responsibilities:

- Implementing security measures such as **firewalls, VPNs, and intrusion detection systems (IDS)**.

- Conducting **risk assessments** and **security audits**.
- Ensuring compliance with security regulations and industry standards.

📌 **Skills Required:**

- Proficiency in **network security, firewall configuration**, and **cloud security**.
- Familiarity with security tools such as **firewalls, VPNs, IDS/IPS**, and **antivirus software**.
- Strong **problem-solving skills** and the ability to think like an attacker.

D. Incident Responder

Incident responders are the first line of defense when a cyberattack occurs. They work to **contain the damage** from incidents, analyze how the attack happened, and help to **prevent future attacks**.

Key Responsibilities:

- Responding to active security incidents (e.g., malware infections, data breaches).
- Analyzing and investigating the **root cause** of incidents.
- Coordinating with teams to implement **remediation measures** and prevent similar attacks.

📌 **Skills Required:**

- Deep knowledge of **incident response protocols** and **forensics tools**.
- Strong understanding of **network traffic analysis** and **malware analysis**.

- Experience with **security frameworks** like **NIST** or **ISO 27001**.

2. Cybersecurity Certifications: CEH, CISSP, Security+, OSCP

Certifications play a **crucial role** in the cybersecurity industry, as they validate your skills and knowledge to potential employers. Some certifications are geared toward **entry-level professionals**, while others are intended for **advanced practitioners**.

A. Certified Ethical Hacker (CEH)

The **CEH** certification is one of the most recognized certifications for penetration testers and ethical hackers. It covers a wide range of topics related to **ethical hacking**, including **penetration testing tools, techniques**, and **network security**.

📌 **Recommended For:**

- Penetration testers, ethical hackers, and security analysts.

B. Certified Information Systems Security Professional (CISSP)

The **CISSP** is an advanced-level certification designed for professionals involved in **information security management**, including security engineers and architects. It's recognized worldwide as a **benchmark for senior security professionals**.

240

📌 **Recommended For:**

- Security managers, security architects, and CISOs (Chief Information Security Officers).

C. CompTIA Security+

Security+ is an excellent entry-level certification for those new to cybersecurity. It covers **network security**, **cryptography**, **threat management**, and more.

📌 **Recommended For:**

- Entry-level cybersecurity professionals, security analysts, and IT professionals.

D. Offensive Security Certified Professional (OSCP)

The **OSCP** is a highly regarded certification for those who want to demonstrate their skills in **penetration testing** and **ethical hacking**. It focuses on hands-on assessments and practical skills in attacking and defending networks and systems.

📌 **Recommended For:**

- Penetration testers, ethical hackers, and anyone looking to prove their ability to **exploit vulnerabilities**.

3. How to Build Hands-On Skills and Create a Cybersecurity Portfolio

Building practical, hands-on skills is critical in cybersecurity. Employers want to see that you can apply your knowledge in **real-world scenarios**.

A. Build a Home Lab

One of the best ways to gain hands-on experience is by creating a **cybersecurity lab** at home. This can include:

- Setting up virtual machines for testing.
- Simulating penetration tests on your own devices.
- Experimenting with security tools like **Kali Linux**, **Wireshark**, and **Metasploit**.

📌 **Example:**
A beginner might set up a **Kali Linux VM** and practice basic penetration testing techniques like **network sniffing**, **password cracking**, and **exploiting vulnerabilities**.

B. Participate in Capture the Flag (CTF) Challenges

CTFs are competitive events where participants solve security puzzles and challenges to test their hacking skills. These events often simulate real-world cyber attacks and are a great way to improve your skills.

📌 **Example:**
Platforms like **Hack The Box**, **TryHackMe**, and **CTF**

competitions offer great opportunities to hone your penetration testing and incident response skills.

C. Create a Cybersecurity Portfolio

Building a **cybersecurity portfolio** allows you to showcase your skills to potential employers. Include:

- **Details of your projects**, such as penetration tests, vulnerability assessments, and security audits.
- **Write blog posts** or articles about the latest security trends and tools you've used.
- **Document your CTF wins** and any certifications or practical experience you've accumulated.

 **Example:**
You could create a portfolio website where you demonstrate the **penetration tests** you've conducted on your own devices or offer **write-ups** of successful CTF challenges.

Key Takeaways

✔ **Cybersecurity offers a wide range of career paths**: from penetration testing to security engineering and incident response.

✔ **Certifications** such as **CEH, CISSP, Security+**, and **OSCP** can help open doors in the cybersecurity field.

✔ **Hands-on skills** are essential for success in cybersecurity—build a lab, participate in CTFs, and create a portfolio to demonstrate your skills.

✔ **Continuous learning** and **real-world experience** are the keys to success in this ever-evolving field.

Next Chapter: The Future of Cybersecurity — Artificial Intelligence, Quantum Computing, and Beyond

In **Chapter 27**, we'll explore how **AI, quantum computing,** and other emerging technologies will reshape the **future of cybersecurity** and present **new challenges**.

🚀 **Get ready for the next frontier of cybersecurity technology!**

CHAPTER 27

Final Thoughts: The Future of Cybersecurity

Introduction

The world of cybersecurity is constantly evolving, with new technologies, strategies, and threats emerging every day. In the coming decade, the **cybersecurity landscape will be drastically reshaped** by advances in **artificial intelligence (AI)**, **quantum computing**, and **automation**. As **cyber threats** become more sophisticated, it's crucial for individuals and organizations to stay ahead of the curve.

In this final chapter, we will explore:

- **What cybersecurity will look like in the next decade** – Key trends and predictions.
- **How AI, quantum computing, and automation will change the landscape** – The technologies that will drive future security strategies.
- **Actionable steps to stay cyber-aware and secure** in an evolving digital world.

By the end of this chapter, you will have a clear understanding of **how cybersecurity will evolve** and how you can **adapt to stay protected** in the years to come.

---

1. What Cybersecurity Will Look Like in the Next Decade

A. The Rise of AI-Driven Security

In the next decade, **artificial intelligence** will play an even more central role in **cybersecurity**. AI will not only help in **automating security tasks** but also in **predicting threats** and **responding faster** to attacks. Here's how:

1 **Proactive Threat Detection:** AI systems will **analyze massive amounts of data** to detect patterns and identify threats before they occur, rather than just reacting to them.
2 **AI-Enhanced Incident Response:** AI will automate responses to incidents, reducing **response times** and allowing human analysts to focus on complex tasks.
3 **Personalized Security Measures:** AI will tailor **security protocols** to individual behaviors and environments, providing more **adaptive and dynamic protection**.

📌 **Example:** AI-driven platforms will be able to detect **zero-day vulnerabilities** (previously unknown security flaws) much faster than human security teams, **remediating threats** before they cause damage.

B. Cybersecurity as a Service (CaaS)

As businesses move more operations to the cloud and adopt **remote work models**, **cybersecurity** will shift from traditional in-house models to **Cloud-based Security-as-a-Service (CaaS)**. This model allows businesses to:

- **Outsource cybersecurity to experts**, reducing costs and ensuring access to the latest technologies.
- **Adopt scalable, cloud-based security solutions** that can adapt to their growing needs.
- **Enhance collaboration** between various cybersecurity service providers, improving overall defense.

246

📌 **Example:**
Organizations will increasingly rely on **third-party security providers** to offer cloud-based protection solutions, enabling faster deployments and reducing the burden on internal teams.

C. The Ongoing Battle Against Ransomware

Ransomware attacks will continue to be a **major cybersecurity threat** in the next decade. However, as organizations adopt more advanced **defensive strategies** like **AI, machine learning**, and **endpoint detection and response (EDR)**, the **battle against ransomware** will evolve.

1. **Improved Ransomware Detection**: AI and machine learning will help detect **ransomware behaviors** before the malware executes, preventing encryption of files.
2. **Data Backup and Recovery**: Organizations will invest more in **backup solutions** and **cloud storage** that provide **instant recovery** from ransomware attacks without paying ransoms.

📌 **Example:**
As ransomware attacks increase in sophistication, organizations will **automate threat detection** and **backup processes** to quickly recover from incidents.

2. How AI, Quantum Computing, and Automation Will Change the Landscape

A. The Role of Artificial Intelligence in Cybersecurity

AI will transform **cybersecurity** by enabling **faster decision-making**, **automated threat detection**, and **dynamic defense mechanisms**. Over the next decade, AI will:

1. **Analyze Behavioral Data:** AI will become more adept at identifying **anomalous behavior** and detecting **advanced persistent threats (APTs)** by analyzing the behaviors of users, networks, and devices.
2. **Automate Security Processes:** Routine tasks such as **vulnerability scanning**, **incident response**, and **patch management** will be automated using AI, reducing human error and freeing up cybersecurity professionals to focus on more complex threats.

📌   **Example:**
AI systems will analyze **network traffic** in real-time, detect potential breaches, and automatically isolate **compromised systems**, reducing response times significantly.

B. Quantum Computing: The Double-Edged Sword

Quantum computing presents both a **massive opportunity** and a **significant threat** to cybersecurity. In the next decade, **quantum computers** will have the ability to break current

248

encryption methods, potentially rendering many traditional security protocols obsolete.

Opportunities:

- **Quantum encryption** methods, like **quantum key distribution (QKD)**, will emerge, making communications **unbreakable** by even the most advanced quantum computers.
- Quantum computers can also **accelerate cryptographic processes**, leading to **stronger and faster encryption techniques**.

Threats:

- **Quantum decryption** could break **RSA encryption**, the backbone of internet security today, exposing private data at a massive scale.

📌 **Example:** Organizations will begin adopting **quantum-resistant algorithms** to future-proof their cybersecurity defenses and ensure that they remain secure as quantum computing evolves.

C. Automation in Cybersecurity

The growing complexity of cybersecurity challenges will lead to **increased automation** in the next decade. Automation will help organizations **scale their security efforts** and respond faster to threats.

1 **Automated Threat Detection and Response**: AI-powered automation will enable **real-time responses** to

detected threats without requiring human intervention. 2 **Security Orchestration, Automation, and Response (SOAR)** tools will integrate various security systems, making **security operations more efficient** and streamlined.

📌 **Example:** Automated systems will detect malware on an endpoint, **isolate the compromised system**, and **remediate the issue** without needing human action, allowing organizations to **focus on strategic tasks**.

---

3. Actionable Steps to Stay Cyber-Aware and Secure in an Evolving Digital World

As we look to the future, it's essential for both individuals and organizations to **adapt** and **stay proactive** in the ever-changing digital landscape. Here's how you can stay **cyber-aware and secure** in the next decade:

✅ For Individuals:

1 **Educate Yourself on Emerging Technologies**: Stay informed about **AI, blockchain**, and **quantum computing** and how they impact cybersecurity.
2 **Use Strong Passwords and Multi-Factor Authentication**: Even in the face of emerging threats, simple security practices like using **MFA** can provide substantial protection.
3 **Stay Up to Date on Cybersecurity Threats**: Follow cybersecurity news, subscribe to threat intelligence platforms, and be aware of **common scams** and **phishing tactics**.

4 **Regularly Update Software and Devices**: Ensure your **devices are patched** with the latest security updates, especially as **zero-day vulnerabilities** and attacks evolve.

✓ For Organizations:

1 **Invest in AI and Automation**: Adopt **AI-driven security tools** to **detect and respond to threats faster**.
2 **Implement Zero Trust Security Models**: Don't trust any device or user by default; continuously verify every request to access resources.
3 **Prepare for Quantum Computing**: Begin transitioning to **quantum-safe encryption** and **quantum-resistant protocols**.
4 **Cybersecurity Training**: Educate your employees on emerging threats and best practices for security to minimize human error.

Key Takeaways

✔ **The next decade will bring significant changes** in cybersecurity, driven by **AI, quantum computing, and automation**.

✔ **AI will transform threat detection, response times**, and incident management.

✔ **Quantum computing poses both a challenge and an opportunity** for encryption, requiring the adoption of **quantum-resistant security measures**.

✔ **Automation** will reduce response times and human error, making cybersecurity systems more **efficient and scalable**.

✔ **Individuals and organizations must stay proactive** by

adapting to new technologies, securing their devices, and **educating themselves** on emerging threats.

Final Thought

Cybersecurity will continue to evolve, but the fundamentals of **education, proactive defense**, and **adaptation** will remain key. By staying informed, adopting new technologies, and embracing change, we can ensure a **secure digital future** in an increasingly complex world.

🚀 **The future of cybersecurity is bright, but it's up to all of us to make it safe!**

www.ingramcontent.com/pod-product-compliance
Lightning Source LLC
LaVergne TN
LVHW022339060326
832902LV00022B/4129